G.L. A

# 'V & W' CLASS DESTROYERS 1917–1945

# 'V & W' CLASS DESTROYERS 1917-1945

Antony Preston

MACDONALD : LONDON

First published in 1971 by
Macdonald & Co. (Publishers) Ltd.,
St. Giles House, 49 Poland Street, London, W.1
Printed in Great Britain by
Hazell Watson & Viney Ltd.,
Aylesbury, Bucks

Dedication  *To my Wife*

# CONTENTS

## PART ONE

### INTRODUCTION

## PART TWO

### APPENDICES

# ACKNOWLEDGMENTS

The author wishes to acknowledge his great debt to all those correspondents who supplied him with reminiscences and technical advice from their service in 'V & W' destroyers, particularly Mr. P. E. Robinson of Deal and many others who helped to recreate the picture for him.

I must also thank my colleagues at the National Maritime Museum for their unstinting help, both in locating material and in checking the text. In this context I must also thank Rear-Admiral P. W. Brock, a Trustee of the Museum, who gave up much of his valuable time to check the details of 'Pozzuoli Sunday'. My thanks are also due to the staffs of the Imperial War Museum, the Naval Historical Branch, the Historical Sections of the Royal Australian Navy, H.M.S. *Vernon* and H.M.S. *Excellent*, all of whom willingly located some obscure facts, figures and photographs.

No acknowledgments in a book on modern British warships would be complete without a tribute to Trevor Lenton and Jim Colledge, who both allowed me to quote from their voluminous records, as did Arnold Hague and Fred Dittmar. Finally, remember the ships themselves, for it is what they did between 1917 and 1945 which made this book worth writing.

# PART ONE

# INTRODUCTION

To those who served in the Royal Navies of World War II no excuse is needed for this memorial to the 'Vs' and 'Ws'. These veterans of the Kaiser's War saw some of the most arduous service imaginable, and although the youngest of them was 15 years old in 1939 and the oldest had been laid down 23 years before, many were still in service in 1945. They fought as fleet destroyers and as convoy escorts from the Arctic Circle to the Far East, and one out of four was lost in action.

The 'V & W' destroyers were in a sense the Dreadnoughts of destroyer design, with heavier armament and better seaworthiness than any of their contemporaries. They remained the finest destroyers afloat for many years and left their mark on designs built all over the world, and indeed every destroyer afloat today owes something in layout to them. For nearly 20 years the Royal Navy continued to build nothing more than slightly improved versions as standard fleet destroyers.

Purists may question the inclusion of the *Shakespeare* and *Scott* class flotilla leaders in a study of 'V & W' boats, but as you will see, the *Shakespeare* was a Thornycroft design to meet the original 1916 requirement for a destroyer leader, and with the very similar *Scott* type shared a common ancestry with the 'V' boats.

From 1918 these sturdy little ships became a familiar sight to sailors, first in the North Sea, as far north as the dreary expanse of Scapa Flow. Their unmistakable trademark was their combination of one thick funnel and one thin of unequal height and when peace came the 'V & W' boats made their appearance farther afield. By the 1930s their silhouette was known from Home waters to the China Station, and a generation of destroyermen had served in them. Virtually every officer and rating who spent any time in destroyers was sent to a 'V' or 'W' sooner or later. Strange as it may seem, Andrew Cunningham, the most famous destroyer officer of all, never commanded one; the greatest destroyer specialist managed somehow to avoid a spell in the Navy's most popular destroyers, although he did command the leader *Wallace*.

Popularity is the keynote of the 'V & W' reputation, for everyone remembers them with affection. Even when they were old, 'they rattled, but they still went'. They grew weary and overcrowded, but nobody had any doubts about their weatherliness. Their outline, however changed by a variety of wartime alterations, was always a welcome sight to the men sailing in Atlantic convoys.

Yet one must also think of these destroyers in their former glory, when they were the latest and largest of the scores of destroyers which put to sea with the Grand Fleet during all its fruitless sweeps. The 'V & W' destroyer was a link with the days of large flotillas and dreadnought battle squadrons. Their shortcomings must be judged against the prevailing standards of their day. Even so, they proved sturdier than many a later destroyer. More than one officer found that he couldn't handle other ships with the same confidence, as newer ships' plating had a habit of buckling more easily.[1] Their machinery was simple and reliable, and their manoeuvrability was exceptional.

Today, there is not a single 'V & W' destroyer hull in existence anywhere in the world. A few South American destroyers modelled on the *Scott* type leaders may still be afloat, but none of the 67 'V & W' boats has survived. This short history cannot attempt to re-create the atmosphere of the days when they served, nor can it cover every episode in their illustrious history, but it does draw on personal reminiscences and official records to show what remarkable warships they were. In relation to their contemporaries they are without doubt the Royal Navy's finest destroyers.

1. To save weight under Washington treaty limitations, the frames of later destroyers were more widely spaced, with the result that plating 'dished' more easily.

# Chapter 1

# DESIGN HISTORY

THE 'V & W' design was conceived in the early months of 1916, at a time when the Allies were conscious that the outcome of the War was not clear. The Grand Fleet was unable to get to grips with the enemy it had been designed to fight, and vast armies of French and British soldiers were bogged down in the mud of the Western Front. Minor successes in other theatres of war had been offset by the stalemate in the west; Imperial forces were in trouble in Gallipoli, in Mesopotamia and in East Africa, but all the Allies' resources had to be devoted to building up their strength to overcome the main German forces in Flanders.

Although the Grand Fleet and other Allied naval forces had not suffered the heavy losses which characterized land warfare, a sense of frustration and impotence was present to a certain degree. Merchant ship losses were rising steadily as the German U-boats perfected their tactics against commerce, but British shipyards at this time continued to give priority to warship production in order to increase the chances of a crushing naval victory in the North Sea. In particular destroyers had proved most useful craft, with their powerful armament and high speed, and naval shipbuilders were all fully committed to turning them out. Since the outbreak of war more than 160 destroyers and flotilla leaders had been ordered (excluding foreign vessels taken over).

In 1915 and 1916 destroyer construction for the Grand Fleet was concentrated on the Admiralty-designed 'R' class, sturdy 3-funnellers which were modelled on the preceding 'M' class. The 'M' boats had been designed before the outbreak of war, and by a policy of repetitive production the Admiralty had been able to boost output of destroyers. The standard 3-funnelled destroyers with the Grand Fleet were an efficient type which compared well with their foreign counterparts in seaworthiness and armament. By the end of May 1916, on the eve of the Battle of Jutland, some 60 'M' class were based in the North Sea, divided between the main fleet base at Scapa Flow, the battle-cruisers at Rosyth, and the Harwich Force.

Early in 1916 the Admiralty submitted a requirement to the Director of Naval Construction calling for a larger type of leader to spearhead the flotillas of 'R' boats then building. This need was due to the expected ability of the 'Rs' to maintain higher speeds than the existing leaders; the introduction of geared turbines promised a great improvement over the direct-drive steam turbines in the *Lightfoot* and *Gabriel* type leaders. Furthermore, the 'Rs' and 'Ms' and their leaders were proving to be on the light side for hard driving in rough weather.

What was needed was a considerably bigger hull with higher free-board; this would give the leader room for a heavier gun armament (an important consideration for a vessel intended to lead destroyer attacks) and allow a higher speed. Two were ordered in April 1916, to be armed with four 4-inch quick-firing guns in superimposed positions forward and aft; in one stroke gun armament went up by 25 per cent, with better command for all weapons.[1] The torpedo armament comprised four 21-inch tubes in two twin mountings, as in existing destroyers. Three more vessels were ordered in July 1916, but as a result of the lessons learned at Jutland an Admiralty order in October increased the armament of the fifth ship, *Vampire*, to two sets of triple tubes, thus putting her on a par with the newest German destroyers.[2]

The first two started life as the *Malcolm* and *Montrose*, named after Scottish heroes of old (possibly because they were building on the Clyde), but the Admiralty was anxious to continue the alphabetical system of class names, as destroyer names had already reached 'S', 'T' and 'U' it was decided to allocate 'V' names; and so *Montrose* became *Valkyrie* and *Malcolm* became *Valorous* in July 1916, early plans showing both sets of names.

When the novelty of the design is considered, and the lack of mass-

1. Despite the increase in size and gun power the estimated cost of the new leader (£200,000) was £40,000 less than the *Lightfoot* type and 25 per cent cheaper to run.

2. The new triple torpedo-tube was lighter than the old pattern of twin tube.

production methods, it was no mean feat of Denny's to launch the prototypes in nine and a half and eleven and a half months respectively. Fitting-out took just over three months for each ship, and *Valkyrie* beat her sister into service by two months to commission as the leader of the 10th Destroyer Flotilla on 6 June 1917; ten days later she finished her trials and left to join the Harwich Force. Three days after the *Valkyrie's* commissioning Cammell Laird's yard at Birkenhead turned out their first 'V' leader, *Valentine*, earmarked for the Battle Cruiser Force and the 13th Flotilla. By an odd quirk of fate this vessel was destined to be the longest-lived of all the 'Vs' and 'Ws', for she was pressed into service in World War II and in spite of being an early loss, her hull remained in existence until 1953, a life-span of thirty-seven years.

While the 'V' class design was still under consideration in April 1916, John Thornycroft & Son had submitted their own design for the new leader, a considerably larger vessel costing an estimated £275,000 as against £200,000 for each 'V' boat, but carrying the prodigious armament of six 4-inch or five 5-inch guns. Although this design was rejected in favour of the smaller design it did meet a separate requirement for an even larger leader which would probably become necessary if destroyer speeds continued to rise to meet operational requirements.

As the 5-inch gun would have to be designed and tested, a time-saving suggestion to modify the Army-pattern 4·7-inch field gun was adopted. Despite the drawback of using separate shells and cartridges the simplicity of the weapon and the increase in shell weight from 32 lb. to 45 lb., fully justified the change from the 4-inch gun. Approval was given for signing contracts for two vessels immediately, a third was ordered in April 1917 and four more in mid-March 1918. The Admiralty order of October 1916 specifying triple torpedo-tubes for the *Vampire* applied to all new leaders;[1] so the whole class was completed with the new scale of armament.

The requirement for a larger leader emanated from Admiral Jellicoe, Commander-in-Chief of the Grant Fleet, and an Admiralty design had been prepared for approval in the same month as the

1. This order also covered the replacement of two 2-pounder pom-poms by a single high-angle 3-inch gun.

Thornycroft 'V'-equivalent was submitted. An initial order for one (to be named *Scott*) was placed with Cammell Laird immediately, but alterations to incorporate features of the Thornycroft design were forwarded to the builders three months later. In common with the *Vampire* and the two Thornycroft leaders on the stocks the torpedo and high-angle gun armament were altered in October 1916, and the *Scott* became an Admiralty version of the Thornycroft design in all respects.

There was similar pressure from the Fleet for larger fleet destroyers to counter rumours of new powerful German destroyers, although post-war evidence showed that these were false alarms. These fears were nonetheless compelling, and the Admiralty wisely decided to save time by adapting the 'V' leader's hull as an ordinary fleet destroyer, simplifying internal accommodation and bridge signalling facilities but otherwise duplicating the design to save time and simplify construction. The first order for twenty-one boats was placed in June 1916, with four more in August; these became the original 'V' class, and were followed by a repeat order for twenty-five, known as the 'W' class. These differed only in having the same torpedo armament as the new leaders, two sets of triple tubes.

The original approach to the design of the new destroyers was a reasonably cautious one, for they violated all the canons of destroyer design in carrying their 4-inch guns high above the waterline. With this top weight in mind the designers felt compelled to limit the number of torpedo-tubes to four, until the introduction of a new lightweight triple tube. However, they had an ample margin of stability, and when the question of increasing the gun armament came under consideration the behaviour of the 'Vs' and 'Ws' was so good that a modified class was given the 4·7-inch guns already fitted in the leaders. This was a great success, and the 'Modified Ws' remained in front line service for years on account of their armament being almost on a par with destroyers built up to fifteen years later.[1]

The second group of modified boats was slightly different, for the boilers were rearranged, making the forefunnel thicker than the after

1. See Ship's Cover Adm 138/578, comment by D.N.C. on 'Modified Ws' being worth retaining after 1933, whereas the 4-inch gunned boats would have to be scrapped to comply with treaty limitations on total tonnage.

one. The first group retained the familiar silhouette of the 'V & W' classes, but could be distinguished by the heavier bulk of the 4·7-inch guns. Owing to the two groups being ordered in January and April 1918 the majority were cancelled after the Armistice, and only seven of each type were completed, in some cases years later; some of the cancelled vessels were launched to clear slips and were hopefully hawked about to foreign buyers before scrapping. In many cases the machinery was sold off for use in other ships or as static plant.

Looking back, one wonders what combination of factors made the 'V & W' design so successful. We have seen how well their increased gun power and performance compared with previous destroyers, but the 'V & W' boats had something more : the detailed design work was good, and so the major improvements were properly evaluated. The paradoxical answer is that the design of the 'Vs' and 'Ws' was both progressive and conservative; it met an important criterion of any design in not introducing too many innovations, but rather concentrating on new combinations of tried components. Thus their geared turbines had already been well tested in the 'R' class, the superimposed gun had been introduced in the *Seymour* class leaders, and their method of construction used the well-tried transverse framing. Where British destroyer designers looked far ahead was in combining these proven ideas, and the expertise acquired in twenty years of building destroyers, with a larger hull, to accommodate greater armament and seaworthiness. In addition, the D.N.C. had for years insisted on sturdy construction and a good margin of stability as prerequisites for destroyers.

The wisdom of the British decision to build nothing more than a bigger and better edition of what had gone before was not appreciated until after the Armistice, when German destroyers could be examined. For years critics had been claiming that German torpedo-craft were superior in every way to their British opponents, and when it was discovered that the Germans had in fact produced the largest destroyers in the world it seemed pointless to argue further. But the postwar tests on surrendered German destroyers proved exactly the opposite, for in nearly all respects British destroyers were more battle-worthy. True, the Germans had produced the *S.113* and *V.116* classes with four 5·9-inch guns, but they were top-heavy, mechanically unreliable and poor seaboats. The Germans had the same experience in World War II with their so-called 'Narvik' types, again armed with 5·9-inch guns, and likewise top-heavy and unhappy in bad weather. The Germans' liking for a heavy gun armament seems to have stemmed from a shortage of light cruisers, but the hybrid light cruiser-cum-destroyer which resulted lacked the virtues of either type.

The weakness of the 5·9-inch gun was, apart from the increase in top weight which affected stability, the weight of the ammunition to be handled. The main advantage of smaller German destroyers apparently lay in the 4·1-inch gun, which was considerably lighter than the Mark V 4-inch and had another 20 degrees elevation; however, this was cancelled out by the lower freeboard in all classes of German destroyers, compared with British destroyers of equal tonnage.

After exhaustive tests in 1919 the D.N.C. was able to report that the superimposed guns of the 'Vs' and 'Ws' made them superior to the largest German destroyers.[1] The following report from Commander England of the *Vivien* about July 1919 shows what this superiority meant in practice :

'I escorted *B.98* (1,374 tons, 321 ft. 6 ins. long) to sea on a mail trip to Germany (carrying mails for interned German ships at Scapa). The wind was S.E. 6–7 with a rough sea. I worked up from 10 to 20 knots by signal and formed the opinion that when steaming to windward above 15 knots she compared very unfavourably with my ship, owing to the amount of water shipped. So much so that on arrival at the departure point I was unable for a long time to get a signal to her to ease down. I considered her to be incapable of fighting at this speed, though my own ship could have been fought comfortably with the exception of No. 1 gun. On the upper bridge *Vivien* was dry and I did not find it necessary to wear an oilskin.'[2]

One can see what the *Vivien*'s C.O. meant, for the British boat carried her guns, tubes and personnel much higher out of the water, and must have proved superior in action; even the smaller 'S' class showed a similar superiority over German craft of the same tonnage. One can

1. Adm 138/621—Ship's Cover relating to German T.B.Ds.
2. Adm 138/621—ibid.

carry this even further, for a 'Modified W' could have been a match for a 1914 light cruiser of the *Arethusa* type. Her 4·7-inch guns, and tubes could have been fought in weather which would have neutralized the advantage of the cruiser's 6-inch guns, since the 4,000-ton *Arethusa* had less stability and freeboard.

# Chapter 2

# SERVICE IN WORLD WAR I

As was to be expected the new 'V' leaders were allocated to North Sea flotillas, where the going was hardest. By late summer 1917 all five were leading flotillas, with the *Shakespeare* and the first five ordinary 'Vs' due to join in the autumn. By the spring of 1918 the shipyards' output was rising, and thirty of the new boats were in service, with seven due to complete within weeks. But the toll of war service was high; the North Sea was thick with German and British mines, and it was not long before they made their presence felt.

The *Valkyrie* had been with the 10th Flotilla of the Harwich Force nearly six months, and had carried out most of the offensive sweeps and convoy runs which were the lot of the Harwich destroyers. On a typical 'beef run' she and a division of four 'R' class boats were guarding the southern flank of a convoy outward bound to the Hook of Holland, while another leader, the *Nimrod*, and four more destroyers were stationed to the north. Their orders were to escort the convoy to Dutch territorial waters and then to pick up a homeward bound convoy, but unlike so many similar routine operations, this one did not go according to plan.

At about 22.15 on the night of 22 December 1917 *Valkyrie* and her division were zigzagging at fourteen and a half knots, when a violent explosion was heard, followed by a second. Commander Burges Watson in the *Tempest* lost sight of his leader but soon found her, shrouded in steam. Burges Watson immediately ordered the rest of the division to stop and pick up survivors, as it was soon clear that they were in a minefield. For a time it looked as if the *Valkyrie* was sinking, but the very first 'V & W' showed how stoutly she was built, and the *Sylph* was ordered to stand by for towing. The delay was agonizing; over an hour after the explosion the *Sylph*'s medical officer was still dealing with badly scalded and burnt men in *Valkyrie*'s engine-room, and towing had not begun.

In the meantime, the convoy had continued to the Hook without incident, and its escorting destroyers dispersed to a pre-arranged rendezvous three miles north of the Maas Light Buoy in order to pick up the fresh convoy. At 01.30 on the morning of 23 December the *Surprise* joined the *Nimrod, Radiant* and *Torrent* waiting in the vicinity of the light buoy for the convoy, but not daring to heave to for fear of submarine attack. When the *Tornado* rejoined half an hour later the division (excluding *Nimrod*, which waited for the convoy) formed in line ahead and steamed south towards the buoy. Suddenly the sickening thud of a heavy explosion brought the *Torrent* to a halt, heeling over within minutes. The *Surprise* turned back immediately to render assistance, but the *Torrent* was going down so fast that she could not get alongside, and the *Tornado* had to come up astern on the other side. The *Radiant* was ordered to stand clear and carry out a search for any U-boat, a decision which was to prove a great blessing in view of what was about to happen.

While the *Surprise* and the *Tornado* were rescuing survivors from the *Torrent*, the stricken ship was shattered by a second explosion, and sank immediately. Both the rescuing ships stood clear, and *Tornado* went ahead to join the *Radiant*, but while the *Surprise* was trying to recover her whaler and some carley floats there was an explosion under her bridge. Commander Thompson was blown overboard, but had the good fortune to be picked up by his own whaler.

One must remember that this succession of disasters was taking place in enemy waters, and it was not clear whether the division had blundered into a German minefield or had possibly fallen foul of an able U-boat commander of the calibre of Otto Weddigen. Despite the fact that a fourth and fifth explosion were seen and heard from the direction in which the *Tornado* had been heading, almost nobody believed that mines were responsible. It seems rather surprising, but at the Court of Enquiry all surviving officers but one seriously maintained that a single U-boat had probably fired torpedoes.[1] After the

1. Adm 137/3707—Ship Histories (P.R.O.), which contains the proceedings of the Court of Enquiry.

Armistice, the German minefield charts showed that the whole area was densely sown with mines, and there can be no doubt that all three ships were mined.

Whatever the reason, all knew that the situation was desperate; only one destroyer out of four remained, and she would probably be sunk with equal ease. Nobody would have blamed the *Radiant*'s captain if he had withdrawn, but the destroyers of the Harwich Force had a strong tradition of standing by their flotilla-mates, and, sending an urgent distress-call to the *Nimrod*, he unhesitatingly moved in to rescue the survivors. Sad to tell, only one survivor from the *Tornado* was picked up, and when the *Radiant* and *Nimrod* returned to Harwich, they brought home only a remnant of the three ships' crews. With a leader badly damaged and three destroyers sunk, the 10th Flotilla had suffered a stunning blow.

Meanwhile the shattered *Valkyrie* had limped home, and it was clear that she would need virtual rebuilding. Over 30 feet of her port bilge keel had been blown away, and there was a hole from there to the upper deck. The forward boiler-room casing and bulkhead had been demolished, and the mast and forefunnel had collapsed; the discovery of a fracture in the upper deck showed how close she had been to breaking her back. After prodigious efforts at Harwich she was ready for a long tow to Chatham, where full repairs could be carried out. The passage took fourteen hours, including a broken tow, and she did not leave Chatham until July the following year. She had seen the last of Harwich, for she then transferred to the 13th Flotilla, based on Rosyth.

Another victim of German mines was the *Warwick*, which had been Vice-Admiral Keyes' flagship at the blocking of Zeebrugge in April 1918. While returning from the second attempt to block Ostend on 10 May she was mined aft and broke her back. The *Velox* was brought alongside to help her afloat, and the two destroyers limped back to Dover. As in the case of the *Valkyrie*, repairs took months, and to the end of her days the *Warwick* bore a scar; she was the only 'V & W' to have a straight stern instead of the normal slightly hollowed type.

The 13th was the first flotilla entirely made up of 'V & Ws', but others were joining the 6th down at Dover, the 11th, 12th and 14th at Scapa, and a new force, the 20th. This group operated as fast minelayers out of Immingham on the Humber, and had a semi-permanent existence under Captain Berwick Curtis, R.N., one of the more unorthodox destroyer captains of his day. In February 1918 four 'Vs', *Vanoc, Vanquisher, Vehement* and *Venturous*, some 'Rs' and some pre-war boats were assigned to Curtis's new command. By the end of 1917 there were seven 'Vs' fitted for minelaying, but the formation of the 20th Flotilla created a specially trained minelaying force; they were frequently detached for convoy duties and general patrol work, and other minelaying destroyers could reinforce them at will, but the nucleus remained.

As minelayers the after twin torpedo-tubes and the quarter-deck 4-inch gun were removed; mine-rails and winches were bolted in place on the upper deck, and screens with painted gun and tubes were rigged to hoodwink any casual observer. As fleet destroyers the missing gun and tubes could be replaced within twelve hours, but some permanent minelayers kept their rails in place all the time.

Captain Taprell Dorling, D.S.O., R.N., better known as 'Taff-rail' has left the only detailed account of the 20th Flotilla's work, which comprised nightly runs into German-controlled waters to sow mines, either the moored 'H' type or a novel infernal machine which was to become better known in another war, the magnetic 'M-sinker'. Minelaying runs were made at high tide to reduce the risk from both enemy and friendly minefields, as dead reckoning could only place minefields within a mile; the difficulties of manoeuvring at night were complicated by the fact that wireless signals were out of the question. The 20th Flotilla operated on the German's doorstep, and had to take its chance with shoals, defensive minefields and enemy patrols; with such a lethal cargo on board minelayers could not even fight, for orders emphatically forbade them to open fire unless fired upon.

Mines were laid in a herring-bone pattern, with each destroyer laying twenty mines on each leg, or forty in all, at a speed which varied from ten to fifteen knots. Any minor hitch such as a mine-sinker jamming on the rails was a frequent hazard which could throw out the whole timetable, while a major accident such as a collision risked the whole force. The flotilla laid some 15,000 mines in enemy waters in 1918, and according to Sir Eric Geddes, First Lord of the Admiralty, these accounted for over 100 vessels.[1]

The 20th Flotilla suffered its only disaster on the night of 2 August 1918, while on its way to lay mines in the Heligoland Bight, steaming in line ahead at high speed. Suddenly, about fifteen minutes before midnight there was a tremendous explosion as the *Vehement*, number five in line, fouled a German mine. In 'Taffrail's' words, 'a brilliant gout of ruby and orange flame mingled with smoke and water standing out of the sea to a height of quite 200 feet . . . an unnerving sight'. When his ship, the *Telemachus* came near the *Vehement*'s stern was still afloat, but everything forward of the funnels had vanished in the detonation of her forward magazine. Miraculously, her captain, Lt.-Cdr. Hammersley-Heenan was blown 400 yards by the blast but not injured, and others had similar escapes.

The *Vehement* might still have made port, for two ships were close at hand to take her in tow, but while this was being arranged the *Ariel* fouled another mine about a quarter of a mile away, and sank within fifteen minutes. The wreck of the *Vehement* was on fire, with stray cordite charges and shells exploding, but when dawn came she was still in tow. Then a bulkhead collapsed and her stern rose higher out of the water; with the wind freshening towing was becoming impossible, so Capt. Berwick Curtis in the *Abdiel* gave the order to sink the wreck. The toughness of the 'Vs' and 'Ws' is demonstrated by the fact that the *Telemachus* fired a number of 4-inch shells at her waterline without any apparent effect; finally the *Vehement* was despatched by a brace of shallow-set depth-charges dropped a few feet away.[2]

Some idea of the strain of wartime service in British destroyers may be gained by a look at the casualty list in mid-summer 1918. Of three 'V & W' boats with the Dover Patrol the *Warwick* was under repair, with a broken back after hitting a mine. The two leaders of the Harwich Force flotilla had been replaced, for the *Valkyrie* had been followed by the *Shakespeare*, mined on 31 May 1918; like her consort she needed extensive repairs, and remained in dockyard

1. Quoted from a speech reported in *The Times*, in *Endless Story* by 'Taffrail', p. 387. See also Grant, *U-Boat Intelligence* (Putnam 1968).
2. The description of this episode is taken from *Endless Story*, see above,

hands for five months. Three of the twelve in the 11th Flotilla were refitting, and the *Vancouver* was under repair after a collision; in the 13th the *Wessex* was damaged from the same cause, and another two were refitting. In all the class suffered four losses, *Scott* and *Vittoria* torpedoed, and *Vehement* and *Verulam* mined between June 1917 and September 1919; in the same period eighteen [1] were in dock for various repairs following collisions or breakdowns.

Although most of the 'V & W' class steamed many miles on anti-submarine patrols, only one of the class was credited with a 'kill' before the Armistice—a record which was to be improved upon in the next war. On 27 July 1918 the *Vanessa* (11th Flotilla, Grand Fleet) finished off *UB. 107* with depth-charges off Scarborough. The U-boat had been sighted by the trawler *Calvia*, and after diving had been detected by the destroyer's hydrophone.

## THE BALTIC CAMPAIGN, 1918–20

The most disgruntled men in the Navy after the Armistice must have been the crews of the 4th Light Cruiser Squadron and the 13th Destroyer Flotilla. One day after the surrender of the High Seas Fleet to Beatty's victorious Grand Fleet the ship which had led the German dreadnoughts into the Firth of Forth, the cruiser *Cardiff*, with four other cruisers, nine destroyers [2] and seven minesweepers left for the Baltic. They had to forego post-war leave, and many of them had not seen wives or families for months, but the need was so urgent that duty came before compassion; the force had orders to support the Estonian, Lithuanian and Latvian governments against Bolshevik aggression, resulting from the state of near-anachy in the Baltic States after the collapse of the Russian war effort in 1917. The situation worsened rather than improved after the collapse of German resistance a year later; Lenin brushed aside the self-determination promised by the Treaty of Brest-Litovsk by claiming that the Baltic

1. *Shakespeare, Valkyrie, Vancouver, Vanity, Vampire, Vanoc, Vega, Vendetta, Versatile, Verulam, Viceroy, Vimiera, Warwick, Vivacious, Westminster, Whirlwind, Wrestler* and *Wessex*.
2. *Valkyrie* (leader), *Verulam, Westminster, Vendetta, Wakeful, Wessex, Windsor, Wolfhound* and *Woolston*.

territories must be 'liberated', and that the Baltic must become a Soviet sea.[1]

This was the real menace of Bolshevism, rather than the vague threat of revolutionary doctrines which is always alleged to have motivated the British intervention in the Baltic; His Majesty's Government was careful to remind the Admiralty that the naval forces sent to the Baltic were not at war with Soviet Russia. The original orders to Rear-Admiral Alexander-Sinclair of the 4th Light Cruiser Squadron were, 'to show the British flag and support British policy as circumstances dictate';[2] and to see that a consignment of arms reached the Estonian and Latvian governments safely, but a 'Bolshevik man-of-war operating off the coast of the Baltic Provinces must be assumed to be doing so with hostile intent. . . .'[3]

The greatest danger, however, was not the Red Fleet but the enormous number of German and Russian mines sown in the Baltic, as well as the navigational hazards. The Baltic is notoriously a shallow sea, and the combination of shoals and poorly charted minefields gave the British forces very little room to manoeuvre. Shortly after their arrival they were given a frightening demonstration of what lay in store for the unwary; while steaming towards Osel (Saaremaa) one of the light criusers, *Cassandra*, was mined and began to sink. In total darkness the *Vendetta* and *Westminster* went alongside the doomed cruiser in turn to take off the crew.

The *Vendetta* went alongside the crippled cruiser's port side; with the water near freezing and the ships rolling heavily it was a fearful hazard to jump from one ship to the other. Despite the darkness and lively motion of both ships only one man missed his footing and fell between the grinding hulls; finally the destroyer sheered off, so crammed with survivors that her flotilla-mates had to take off a number in turn. When the *Westminster* had finished, it was suddenly noticed from the *Vendetta*'s bridge that a man was still left on board, so she closed the *Cassandra* once more. To avoid the risk of damage the *Vendetta*'s captain ordered the man to launch the cruiser's dinghy and cut himself adrift; this expedient was successsful, but the man concerned was promptly put on a charge for failing to abandon ship !

1. *Pravda*, quoted in *Cowan's War*, by Geoffrey Bennett, p. 30.
2. ibid p. 34.          3. ibid p. 34.

The loss of the *Cassandra* did not affect the aims of the Baltic expedition, but the *Cassandra*'s survivors had to be returned to Rosyth. Accordingly, the *Calypso*, which had been damaged when she struck a submerged wreck off Libau (Liepaja), and the *Westminster* and *Verulam*, which had been in collision, were all sent home with the *Cassandra*'s men.

The first brush with the Red Fleet was rather more encouraging. On Boxing Day 1918 most of the officers and men were ashore at Reval (Tallinn) preparing for a banquet given in their honour by the Estonian authorities, when a strange craft was sighted on the horizon and shells began to burst around the harbour. It was the Soviet destroyer *Spartak*, a new and powerful product of Tsarist expenditure on the old Russian Navy, and she had on board no less a personage than F. F. Raskolnikov, a member of the Revolutionary War Soviet of the Baltic Fleet, specially appointed to command on this occasion.

Unfortunately the *Spartak* had been let down badly by her consorts, for the destroyer *Avtroil* had broken down, the *Azard* was out of fuel and the cruiser *Oleg* did not come up in support. Relying on the battleship *Andrei Pervozvanni* to help him out of any trouble Raskolnikov rashly signalled his intention of bombarding Reval single-handed, but his confidence evaporated when he saw the destroyer *Wakeful* leave harbour after raising steam in only fifteen minutes, followed by the cruisers *Calypso* and *Caradoc*.

The *Wakeful* gave chase, firing as she went, and her quarry fled, but suddenly turned sixteen points and stopped with a white flag hoisted. It turned out that she had dispatched a signal a short while before, 'All is lost. I am chased by the English',[1] and had then stripped her rudder and propellers by running over a shoal at high speed.

The Soviet version was disarmingly frank : '. . . . the pursuing British destroyers attaining a speed of thirty-five knots, while the *Spartak* was unable to develop full speed because the crew operated the machinery incorrectly. . . . At about 13.30 hours the blast from the *Spartak*'s forward gun, trained too far aft, knocked down the charthouse, scattered and tore the charts, damaged the bridge and concussed the helmsman, so that the ship's position could not be determined.'[2]

1. See *Cowan's War*, p. 41.  2. See *Cowan's War*, p. 43.

The opportunities of capturing enemy ships intact are rare in modern warfare, but some astute person aboard the *Vendetta* pointed out that the *Spartak* could be looted as a lawful prize. The Soviet vessel appeared to be sinking slowly, and permission was given to remove anything portable; this turned out to be unduly pessimistic, and a large quantity of jewellery and silver was removed without difficulty. This seems hard to believe, but an eye-witness testifies to the fact that the *Vendetta* landed an enormous amount of loot at Port Edgar, which must have gone into the Prize Fund.

One of the *Vendetta*'s engine-room complement had been a mining engineer who had previous experience of pumps and when he examined the *Spartak*'s engine-room he announced the pleasant news that the ship could be kept afloat simply by closing the sea-cocks and starting the pumps. Once this had been done she was towed back to Reval, where the banquet became a victory feast. The British were anxious to catch the *Oleg* as soon as they learnt of the Soviet dispositions, from documents found in the *Spartak*, and the *Vendetta* and *Vortigern* went off to look for her and the destroyer *Avtroil*. No sign of the *Oleg* was seen but the *Avtroil* fell foul of five ships in turn and finally surrendered when she realized that escape was impossible. Apart from two modern destroyers, the British had captured Raskolnikov, who was found hidden under potato bags, and he was later exchanged for no fewer than eighteen British prisoners in Bolshevik hands; the two destroyers were presented to the fledgling Estonian Navy, and served proudly as the *Vambola* and *Lennuk* for some years.

One relic of this encounter outlived both the *Spartak* and the *Avtroil*. While the *Spartak* was being searched, one of the *Vendetta*'s crew noticed that the Soviet ship had a handsome bell. Probably as a result of wartime shortages the *Vendetta* lacked the normal ship's bell, and so the omission was remedied. In the course of time the *Vendetta* was transferred to the Royal Australian Navy, and earned herself a proud record before being scuttled off Sydney Heads in 1948. One can only hope that her bell was preserved, and with it some note of its peculiar pedigree.

The British force could not stay indefinitely as both ships and men were under exceptional strain while operating so far from home, and in January 1919 they were relieved. However, by the time they reached Rosyth on 10 January they could console themselves that an important part of their mission had been accomplished; the Finns were reassured that their security was no longer in danger, and Estonia had been materially helped to establish her independence. When Rear-Admiral Cowan's relieving force took over there was a sound basis for co-operation with the Baltic States and confidence about the role the Royal Navy would play.

Once again the 'Vs' and 'Ws' and the leaders were in the forefront; the cruisers *Caledon* and *Royalist* were accompanied by five 'Vs' and 'Ws' of the 2nd Flotilla. This was a reconstituted flotilla made up largely of units of the old 13th, and the Admiralty had wisely decided that conditions in the Baltic were so severe that the ships should be relieved roughly every six weeks by their flotilla- and squadron-mates. Cowan left the Baltic on 21 February 1919, but only until the spring, when naval operations would become easier. By mid-June Cowan had the whole 1st Flotilla (led by the *Wallace*), sixteen 'V & W' destroyers, as well as the *Campbell* leading part of the 3rd Flotilla, and the 20th Minelaying Flotilla. Later the 1st Flotilla was replaced by the *Spenser* and the 2nd, but Cowan always found work for his destroyers. On 2 June the *Vivacious* and *Voyager* had briefly exchanged fire with two Bolshevik destroyers off Petrograd, followed by a similar action involving the *Versatile*, *Vivacious* and *Walker*. The Reds were not completely supine, and on 9 June Cowan's force at Biorko Sound was nearly surprised by two Soviet destroyers, which had to be chased away by the *Versatile*, *Vivacious* and *Walrus*.

Soviet submarines were also a menace, and the *Watchman* had to drop depth-charges on a submarine which attacked the British submarine *E.40*; three days later the *Vancouver* and *Valorous* had to counter-attack in similar manner. Finally this lethal game of hide-and-seek came to a head when the *Vittoria* was torpedoed off Seskar Island on 31 August 1919 by the Bolshevik submarine *Pantera* (which had attacked *E.40* two months before). This misfortune was followed by another on 4 September, when the *Verulam* hit a British mine off Stirs Point. Cowan remarked that she and the rest of the 2nd Flotilla had 'scarcely yet become accustomed to the difficult conditions of maintaining the patrols under the cramped conditions of manoeuvring space'.[1]

Since movements were so circumscribed, the bulk of the action was seen by destroyers. The following quotation from a diary kept by one of the *Westminster*'s crew gives some idea of the burden placed on the Baltic destoyers :

'With *Vectis, Walpole* and *Valentine*, left harbour, *Walpole* and ourselves making straight for the Estonian coast. Our duties are to patrol the flank of the troops ashore. Bolshevik forts are plainly to be seen, but make no effort to fire at us. During the afternoon an Estonian destroyer suddenly made a quick dash right in under the land, loosed off a few salvoes and as quickly nipped out again. No reply from the shore to this greeting. . . .

'With *Walpole* off Estonian coast; at 16.45 *Walpole* opens fire on battery ashore, keeping up 4-inch shell fire for half an hour or more. Battery returns an accurate fire but falling short. *Walpole* must be anchored just out of range. *Walpole* gets under way and, moving along the coast, opens up a fine bombardment with all guns on what appears to be a factory with tall chimney. We could see the fall of shot and the firing was very good. *Walpole* had further gun practice later but we left the area to escort *E.39* to patrol area. . . .

'*Spenser* signals coming out at 0600 to assist bombardment. We again escort *E.39*, then join up with *Spenser* and *Walpole*. At 1045 we closed up at action stations to do a little bombarding on our own account. *Spenser* ceased fire but *Walpole* continued until *Westminster* opened up. Shore guns now turned from *Walpole* on to us. They gradually got our range but fall of shot was well astern of us. We opened fire at 11,000 yards and selected the tall chimney, which was apparently being used as an observation post. We found the range as 10,800 yards and claimed some hits though the chimney still stood. After a lnal 12 rounds of lyddite we returned to patrol.' [2]

For reasons of expediency the Allies had been forced to make use of a force of 12,000 German troops under Major-General von der Goltz, which had originally been called in by the Finns to suppress a Bolshevik-inspired rebellion. Goltz's 'Iron Division' was allowed to

1. *Cowan's War*, p. 163.
2. *Cowan's War*, pp. 163-4.

A brand new 'V & W' leaving for her trials – *Vanoc* passing Clydebank in 1917.

Two views of *Valhalla*, leader of the 12th Destroyer Flotilla at Scapa in 1918. Note the prominent caging on her funnels, and the bomb thrower just visible to the left of the quarterdeck gun.

The new leader *Valkyrie* limps home to Harwich after hitting a German mine in December 1917. The foremast and funnel are down and there is an enormous hole at the break of the forecastle.

*Scott*, name-ship of her class, photographed at the moment a U-boat's torpedo struck her. With her flotilla she had been engaged in a sweep off the Dutch coast on August 15, 1918, and sank with heavy loss of life.

Another victim of German mines – the *Shakespeare* managed to limp home but, like the *Valkyrie*, she needed extensive repairs. Note the different appearance of the leaders' funnels: whereas the 'V & W' trademark was a combination of one thick and one thin funnel of different heights, the leaders had two equal-sized funnels (flat-sided in Thornycroft vessels).

*Vendetta* and other 'V & W' boats in the destroyer pens at Port Edgar, in the Firth of Forth in 1918 or 1919.

*Vampire* shows off her handsome lines in dry dock *c.* 1918.

A photograph of *Vanoc* during fitting out at John Brown's yard in 1917. Note that some R.N. personnel is already aboard, but the builders' workmen are still in evidence.

*Vanoc's* mine rails and chutes. The mines are dummies, as live mines would have been too dangerous in a builder's yard.

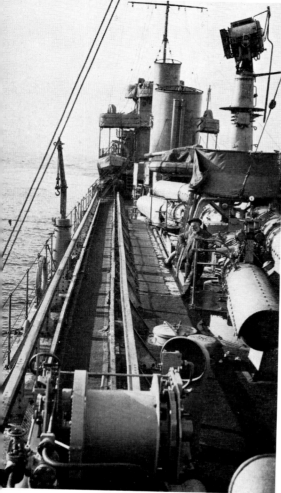

(*Above*) One of the 20th Flotilla minelayers at sea, *Vanquisher*, has her mine rails and chutes camouflaged by a painted canvas screen from the searchlight platform amidships right aft. Note the dirty unkempt appearance, so typical of Grand Fleet destroyers by 1918. Although the patrol work left little time for spit-and-polish, contemporary accounts stress the air of staleness in the G.F. flotillas.

(*Left*) A view along the mine rails of the new 'W' class minelayer *Walker*. Note that the later minelayers had the rails extending forward almost to the whaler, which increased their mine capacity.

(*Above*) One of the 'V' class on trials, probably the Hawthorn Leslie-built *Verulam* or *Versatile*. In Imperial War Museum records she is identified as the *Vanoc*, but the prominent funnel caging makes this impossible.

(*Right*) The *Wrestler* in High Dock, South Shields, after a collision with the battleship *Hindustan* in 1918.

The *Vega* lying alongside at Reval (Tallinn) during the 1919 Baltic Campaign. Note that she has been fitted with a tall pair of aerial 'spreaders' in place of her normal mainmast.

The *Witherington* off St. Tropez on her return from the China Station in 1928.

remain under arms in the belief that it would prove capable of preventing the Soviets from overrunning the Baltic States. However, Goltz saw himself not only as the last German general, with a mission to redeem Prussian military honour, but seriously entertained the hope of setting up a new German empire of the Baltic. The Allies paid dearly for their ignorance of the situation, for as time went on they found that the Iron Division was impossible to control, and too powerful to disarm. The original intention of using the Germans to fight the Reds gave way to a struggle to preserve the new Baltic nations from the Germans. After endless trouble over the Germans' presence in Latvia, the point was reached in October 1919 where they were attacking Riga itself, in defiance of an Allied ultimatum.

The Senior British naval officer at Riga, Captain Berwick Curtis, had the remnants of his 20th (Minelaying) Flotilla and some French ships to support the Latvian Army against a mixed force of Germans and Russian renegades under Bermondt-Avalov. Although the Latvians only numbered some 9,000 against 15,000 disciplined Germans they had the fervour of patriotism, as well as the moral and physical support of the warships to offset the Germans' superiority in weapons and training. In addition, the Latvians received some reinforcements which brought their numbers up to nearly 13,000. Admiral Cowan also despatched the light cruisers *Dragon* and *Cleopatra* and the big minelayer *Princess Margaret* to Riga to strengthen Curtis's hand.

The presence of warships was a factor omitted from the Germans' calculations. Their first intervention was to drive the Germans out of Fort Dünamünde (Daugavgriva) at the mouth of the Dvina (Daugava) River. Then when the Latvian forces repulsed the first German attack on Riga the ships were able to join in effectively. Between 17 and 25 October 1919 the cruisers and the *Venturous* and other vessels of the 20th Flotilla were under fire, but avoided serious damage. These efforts were not enough, for on 3 November Bermondt attacked once more; the cruiser *Dragon*, four 'V & W' destroyers and the French sloops joined the Latvians in eight days and nights of fierce fighting until the Germans finally conceded defeat. At the same time, however, the Germans were faring better in an attack on Libau, where the cruisers *Phaeton* and *Dauntless* and destroyers *Winchester*,

*Whitley, Valorous* and *Wryneck* faced much the same tasks as their sisters at Riga.

At long last Cowan was able to spare some heavy support, in the shape of the monitor *Erebus*, which arrived at Libau on 8 November. All ships joined in counter-battery fire, and on the morning of the 14th the Germans launched their final all-out attack. What followed gave the Germans a salutary lesson in the power of naval gunfire, for the *Erebus* was able to fire over open sights at German infantry at less than 3,000 yards, an event unique in modern warfare. An eye-witness reported that the Iron Division melted away under the shattering blast of 15-inch H.E. shells. The destroyers and cruisers supplied a greater volume of fire from their 4-inch and 6-inch guns, but the margin of victory over defeat was small, for the *Valorous* ran out of ammunition and all the others were running short. The awful destruction caused by the *Erebus* drove the Iron Division away from Libau, and proved to be the final push which overthrew Goltz's Baltic schemes; four days later the Germans asked for an armistice, which was refused, and by the end of the month they had been finally expelled from Latvia.

With winter coming on fast there was little further to be done. Already ships were reporting difficulties with equipment freezing, despite steam heating. The hard-worked destroyers of Cowan's force left in December; they had seen the last of the Baltic, excepting the few who returned on a friendly visit to Copenhagen in May 1920, escorting the battle-cruisers *Hood* and *Tiger*. Although the hard-won independence of Lithuania, Latvia and Estonia was to vanish at the start of the Second World War, their brief taste of self-determination was largely due to the efforts of the Royal Navy during those troubled months of the Baltic intervention, and the whole episode reflects great credit on the officers and men involved.

# Chapter 3

# THE YEARS OF PEACE

## POST-WAR FLOTILLA DEPLOYMENT

IN the spring of 1919 all destroyers were reorganized into new flotillas. The new 1st Flotilla was part of the Atlantic Fleet, with *Wallace* as Captain (D)'s ship and *Valorous* as a divisional leader, with the bulk of the old 11th D.F. The 2nd Flotilla was based at Rosyth and incorporated the old 13th D.F. under the leaders *Spenser* and *Shakespeare*; like the 1st, this flotilla was under strength as long as the Baltic operations continued. The *Campbell* and *Valhalla* were leader and half-leader respectively of the new 3rd Flotilla, also at Rosyth, while the old 20th minelaying flotilla was still in existence.

The new leaders of the *Scott* and *Shakespeare* classes were nearly all in service, but *Malcolm* and *Mackay* were still completing, while the *Rooke* (to be renamed *Broke* in 1921 in honour of Evans's immortal action in 1917) and the *Keppel* were still on the stocks. All the original 'Vs' and 'Ws' had been completed, but only sixteen of the fifty-four 'Modified Ws' ordered in January and April 1918 had been authorized for completion, and none had yet come into service. Work was continued on others for a time, but in September 1919 the last of the laggards was axed.

In 1921 there was a further reorganization, and all flotillas were organized into smaller tactical units comprising one leader and eight destroyers, as the old flotillas had proved too large to handle conveniently. Throughout World War I there had been a tactical problem of how to pass messages rapidly from the leader to sixteen destroyers, even with a half-leader heading the second division and sharing the burden of administration and paper-work. The problem was finally solved by halving the size of flotillas, with the result that by the end of 1921 the new dispositions were as follows:

**1st Flotilla** (Atlantic Fleet)
*Wallace* (Leader)
*Vancouver,\* Velox, Versatile,\* Vortigern,\* Walker,\* Warwick,\* Watchman,\* Whirlwind \**

**2nd Flotilla** (Atlantic Fleet)
*Spenser* (Leader)
*Vanquisher,\* Violent, Vectis, Venetia,\* Viceroy, Viscount, Winchelsea, Wolfhound*

**3rd Flotilla** (Atlantic Fleet)
*Campbell* (Leader)
*Verity, Veteran, Wanderer, Wild Swan, Wishart, Witherington, Wivern, Wolverine*

**4th Flotilla** (Atlantic Fleet)
*Mackay* (Leader)
*Valorous, Vampire, Whitshed, Venomous, Volunteer, Vansittart, Wolsey, Woolston*

**5th Flotilla** (Atlantic Fleet)
*Malcolm* (Leader)
*Vanity, Vendetta, Vivacious,\* Voyager, Walrus,\* Waterhen, Wrestler, Wryneck*

**6th Flotilla** (Atlantic Fleet)
*Shakespeare* (Leader)
*Valhalla, Vega, Vidette, Walpole, Westcott, Wessex, Westminster, Windsor*

**9th Flotilla**
(laid up at Rosyth with reduced complements)
*Bruce* (Leader)
*Douglas* (Leader), *Valentine, Valkyrie, Vanessa, Venturous,\* Verdun, Vesper, Vivien, Whitley*

**7th Flotilla** (Mediterranean Fleet)
*Stuart* (Leader)
*Montrose* (Leader) and twenty 'S' Class

**Miscellaneous**
*Vimiera* (refitting at Chatham); *Vanoc* (in reserve at Devonport)

\* Fitted as minelayer.

36

In 1920 it was decided to increase the torpedo armament of all the early 'V' boats, and as they came into dockyard hands for re-fitting, triple tubes were substituted for the twin tubes. However, the remaining five minelaying 'Vs' *Vanoc, Velox, Versatile, Vancouver* and *Vortigen* did not have the after twin tubes replaced[1] and remained 5-tube boats until the Second World War; others were not altered until five or six years later. Another change in armament authorized was the substitution of a 2-pounder pom-pom for the 3-inch high-angle gun mounted abaft the funnels.[2] As with the triple tubes, it was a long time before all boats were refitted; e.g. when the *Valhalla* was paid off in January 1931 she was the only boat still armed with a 3-inch gun, although her tubes had been altered in 1925.

When not exercising at sea the destroyers of the Atlantic Fleet spent much of their time at Port Edgar, the wartime destroyer base which had been constructed at Port Queensferry in the Firth of Forth. There they lay alongside in the 'pens' in comparative comfort, with electric power laid on from shore and stores available. The victualling system in force for destroyers functioned quite well in a permanent base, with a canteen ashore, but when a flotilla went off on a cruise in home waters the weaknesses became apparent. The destroyers would each draw enough bread and meat for four days, as well as other commodities, but as the 'V & W' boats (in common with older destroyers) had no refrigerator, the amount of perishables which could be carried was small, especially in summer.

On a summer cruise around the South Coast and West Country ports the ship's company could easily be reduced to bully beef and biscuits, with bread bought ashore if they were lucky. On such occasions the depot ship would be absent, which accounted for the breakdown in the system, but to the seaman of today the old victualling system must appear very strange. Each man received a basic ration of bread, meat and potatoes, or if these were not available, bully beef,

1. Others retained their minelaying chutes, but these five were earmarked as destroyer-minelayers in Pink List dispositions.
2. The modified 'Ws' had been completed with two single pom-poms from the outset.

lentils, etc., and tinned milk and cocoa for supper to supplement tinned rabbit or a ration of meat and vegetables.

Each man also received an allowance of money which covered purchases of bacon and other minor luxuries. Each morning the cook of each mess 'fell in' at the butcher's block to receive the mess rations of meat, bread and potatoes; he then prepared the day's dinner for his mess and took it to the galley for cooking. In other words, each mess had its say in how it wanted the food prepared, but the final product depended on how adept the ship's cook might be at preparing a roast and a pie simultaneously. The coxswain kept all the victualling records, and his right-hand man acted as butcher. The meat cage was hung just abaft the foremost funnel, and the butcher would stand at his block, with scales and knife handy, and cleaver in hand, ready to give each mess its meat ration. It should be mentioned here that butchering experience was not a requisite of the job, and if the piece was right for weight, it was handed over regardless of the proportion of bone to meat. The remainder of the meat went back into the meat cage where it was exposed to the preserving effects of sun and wind; after three days it took on a fine weathered look.

By modern standards the living conditions in the 'V & W' classes were spartan, although they compared favourably with older and smaller craft. Water for the galley was pumped up from the freshwater tanks by hand and stored in a tank on the upper deck. Normally in peacetime a wing fuel-tank on either side of the after boiler-room could be cleaned out and used to augment the supply of fresh water, since any time spent at sea produced a shortage. The salt water gravity tank for flushing the 'heads' also had to be filled by means of a hand-pump, and it was the responsibility of the 'captain of the heads' to ensure that this was done each morning.

Seamen and stokers had a crude wash-place under the break of the forecastle, comprising half a dozen tipping basins over a trough, and exposed to the elements. Officers had to depend on a circular tin bath; during the day it was suspended from hooks on the deckhead of the cabin. As a flotilla-leader *Mackay* had the rare luxury of a full-sized bath, but by the 1930s 'some economist' had disconnected the water! The Navy had a word for this sort of thing, 'O.U.N.E.', or Owing to the Urgent Need for Economy, the inevitable preface to all the minor economies enforced by the Admiralty to keep expenses down.

O.U.N.E. meant, for example, that the turbo-generator had to shut down early, hence 'Pipe Down' at 2200 in fleet destroyers, or as a special privilege, 2300 for the leader. However, the Gunner (T)[1] almost invariably wired up a small secondary lighting circuit for the wardroom and officers' cabins, running off the 20-volt batteries used for fire-control circuits. The light was extremely dim, and had to be supplemented by oil lamps. In this respect it is interesting to note that the messdecks had no lighting but sperm oil lamps.

Even after years of service the 'Vs' and 'Ws' stood out from their successors by virtue of their toughness and seaworthiness. By comparison the modern destroyers of the 1930s were described as 'tinny', and the older vessels enjoyed a reputation for mechanical reliability that was not common in the Royal Navy. Their handling was excellent, and even people not accustomed to them found that they turned 'like a London taxi'. One point was held against them : they spoiled one for other destroyers, as one illustrious captain found when he dented a 'Tribal' badly while merely putting her alongside in the manner appropriate to his previous 'V & W' command.

Rear-Admiral Horan has given an interesting account[2] of his first month in command of H.M.S. *Wolsey* in 1922.

'You can well imagine my delight when there came a chit from the Admiralty saying that they had appointed me to "H.M.S. *Wolsey* in command". Now the *Wolsey* was a destroyer I had known well in the Grand Fleet. She had been completed in 1917[3] by that well-known firm of builders of high-speed ships and craft Messrs. John I. Thornycroft and Company of Woolston. . . . Although one of the "W" class destroyers the builders had been allowed a certain amount of latitude with the design of both the hull and the engines,[4] which resulted in giving her a distinctive appearance and a reputation for

1. Torpedomen were responsible for all ships' electrical arrangements until the formation of the Electrical Branch in World War II, a legacy of the pioneering work done by H.M.S. *Vernon*, the Navy's Torpedo School.
2. See *The Nautical Magazine*, Vol. 185 (1961).
3. Actually May 1918 (see Part II).
4. For full particulars of the Thorycroft and standard 'W' class see Part II.

speed. With their extra freeboard and tall funnels the *Wolsey* and her sister ships could be spotted miles off and stood out as "Thornycroft ships" among the rest of the "W" class destroyers.

'On a damp drizzly day in November 1922, I joined her in the Pens at Port Edgar in the Firth of Forth, but to my eyes she was everything a destroyer should be and the Captain I took over from said he had a wonderful ship's company; within a month I was quite convinced that his words were true—in fact I felt that there was literally nothing that the *Wolsey*'s ship's company could not do.

'At once, on joining I was told that the whole flotilla [7th] was going to be stationed at various ports round Ireland but they would be home by Christmas. Quite what we had to do was at the time a bit obscure, but since the signing of the Anglo-Irish Treaty fighting had broken out between the forces of the legally constituted government of Eire and certain dissident elements who were getting money and arms from outside sources. Besides stopping these supplies it seemed the ships of the flotilla would be employed visiting the ports and anchorages which had been ceded to Britain in the Anglo-Irish Treaty.

'Prior to sailing from the Firth of Forth I was told that the *Wolsey* would be stationed at Queenstown (now Cobh) and that we would have as company the *Woolston* which was another Thornycroft-built ship. . . .

'On leaving the Firth of Forth the flotilla shaped course northabout in quite reasonable weather. However, after passing through the Pentland Firth and rounding Cape Wrath there was every sign that we were in for a hard westerly gale. This duly struck us on the run through The Minches but, being in the lee, things were quite comfortable. We went through the Kyle of Loch Alsh during the full strength of the north-going tidal stream, and the way the ships ahead were affected by the current will always remain in my memory—the speed of the flotilla was fifteen knots.

'After passing the Islands of Coll and Tiree we met the full force of the gale which had now gone round to the north-west; this put the sea just abaft the beam, so when passing Skerryvore and Islay, we had an interesting experience in rolling but the way the ship behaved was impressive.

'The run down the Irish Sea was uneventful and by the time we had arrived off Wexford the rest of the flotilla had parted company and *Wolsey* and *Woolston* shaped course for Queenstown. The Senior Naval Officer there, himself an Irishman, was most helpful and explained the situation as he saw it from the information available, which was certainly very sketchy—communications of any kind seemed to be practically non-existent. To remedy this, the *Woolston* was sent to Sligo with orders to look in at some of the anchorages on the way, while we were ordered to Kingstown (now Dun Laoghaire). Here we met a cruiser of the "D" Class and another destroyer; the two destroyers were to act as escort to the cruiser when the latter embarked General Sir Neville Macready when he left Dublin with the last of the British regiments to be stationed in Southern Ireland.

'It was a beautiful Sunday morning when the Viceroy embarked in the cruiser, and as his flag was broken at the masthead, a salute of twenty-one guns was fired. Every vantage point in the harbour was crowded with sightseers, and when we all slipped and proceeded the crowds broke into song "Will ye no come back again?" followed by "God Save the King". It was a touching farewell.

'On parting with the cruiser, the *Wolsey* was ordered to Queenstown. On arrival orders were received to proceed to Galway. I looked forward to going back to the haunts of my youth and revisiting the places in Ireland which the Atlantic Fleet used to frequent before the First World War, and as the weather was good, we set off gaily on our mission. When off the Fastnet one of the big four-funnelled Cunarders passed us steering west; she was a lovely sight as she breasted the long Atlantic swell at well over twenty knots. After rounding the Fastnet we passed the Skelligs and the Blaskets, then sighted Loop Head and early in the morning made Inishmore (Aran Islands) at the entrance to Galway Bay. As we neared Galway it came on thick with a strong south-westerly wind. To get what lee we could I anchored about two cables off the town jetty, landed and called on the harbour master, who seemed to have "the wind up" about something. He arranged for me to call on the Officer Commanding the Troops early next day—neither he nor I were quite sure which faction the officer belonged to!

'Accompanied by the Coxswain, next morning I landed attired in frock coat and sword and made my way to the Railway Station which was the local H.Q. Outside was a guard of twenty-five file whose appearance and arm-drill was of a very high order—they had all served in either the Connaught Rangers or the Munster Fusiliers during the War. It was with relief that I learned that this detachment belonged to "the legitimate government of Ireland". Assisted by a sergeant, the Coxswain was able to obtain a certain amount of Christmas fare for our ship's company; this the Commandant insisted should be looked on as a gift from the Irish Army and was accompanied by an invitation to a Ball to be held on Christmas Day. Whatever had happened in the past was now forgotten and cordial relations had been firmly established as far as the Royal Navy was concerned.

'Christmas Eve dawned with a hard south-westerly blow and driving rain with a falling glass; I did not like the look of the weather. During the dog watches the wind started to veer and the glass steadied, so in anticipation of a blow we got steam on the engines, dropped the second anchor under foot and set anchor watch. As darkness came on the wind increased and became squally, all the time working round to the north-west.

'During the first watch the squalls got worse and heavier, with hail, but careful watch showed that we were holding, and so it was hoped that we would ride it out. But at about 2 a.m. in the middle watch on Christmas Day we were hit by the very father and mother of all the squalls I have ever seen. The ship began to drag. As there was only about a cable to go to the "putty" prompt action was taken. Using half speed ahead and astern on the engines, the stern was turned into the wind; this enabled the "hands" to get on to the forecastle—they could not stand on it before owing to the strength of the wind. One anchor was weighed, but as the ship was getting too close for comfort to the rocks, it was decided to go full speed astern into the wind and drag the other anchor with us. While doing this the seas were coming over the quarter deck and the spray going over the top of the super-imposed gun aft. We must have looked a bit odd! To my surprise the cable held and when it was safe to do so we stopped and weighed the anchor—at any rate we were all safe and in one piece again!

'Being Christmas Day it was decided to get up in the lee of the

Arran Islands and get the motion off the ship so that Christmas dinner could be cooked. It was blowing a regular hurricane and anchor-
ing was out of the question, so we kept underway at slow speed and
had our meals in peace.

'Early next morning we received orders to go to Cahirciveen. By
that time the wind had taken off considerably, but a full-size swell
was running, so away we went. It was a treat to watch the way the
ship rode the long Atlantic seas; we literally disappeared when we
were in the trough between two swells which must have been some-
where about 50 to 60 feet high, but as the sea was long and on the
beam, we hardly shipped a drop of water.

'In the cold grey light of early dawn next day we made the entrance
to the anchorage off Cahirciveen. This is only about 100 yards wide
and faces just west of north. When we arrived the big north-westerly
swell, which had been with us all the way south, was breaking right
across the entrance, so I decided to wait for it to ease a bit and
anchored in Ventry Bay. Towards evening things had quietened
down enough for us to negotiate the breakers so we anchored off
Cahirciveen. It is a snug little harbour but the only place where
there was two cables' swinging room was labelled "Bad holding
ground".

'Next morning (27 December), in frock coat and sword I landed
and was told by a most helpful fisherman where the Commandant
was to be found. After a long walk mostly through fields I found a
sentry who executed a perfect salute with his rifle (he had been in
the Munsters). The Commandant was in bed as there had been some
kind of Christmas party the night before. He accepted my invitation
to return my call next day. On returning on board I found the postmaster and the local bank manager in the ward room. They had
come to ask if I would take the mails to Queenstown and also all the
money that was in the bank, as communications had been completely cut with the blowing up of both road and rail bridges in the
vicinity. This job I undertook to do and reported the fact to the
Senior Naval Officer at Queenstown.

'Punctually the Commandant, accompanied by two other officers,
appeared the next day to return my call. At about the same time, the
postmaster and the bank manager appeared with the mail and the

money bags. I entertained the officers in my cabin while the others were looked after in the wardroom and their precious cargoes were locked away in the after magazine. When the officers left they were seen over the side with the usual ceremony suitable for the occasion, but we noticed that, as their boat shoved off all three of them took their pistols from their cowboy-type holsters and laid them on the thwarts alongside them. After that we felt relieved.

'During the afternoon the weather began to "turn sour"; it came on to blow from the west accompanied by heavy drizzle and the glass started to fall with some rapidity. By 4 p.m. things were very ominous so it was decided that, rather than being caught on bad holding ground, we would get to sea and ride it out there.

'As darkness was falling we weighed and had a look at the entrance. It was not a nice sight; the swell was breaking right across it, but it was noticed that during a period of fifteen waves there seemed to be a lull about the seventh, eighth and ninth. Accordingly we timed it so that we would go through during this lull. We approached at fifteen knots and went from what was practically flat calm to a full Atlantic sea in about a ship's length. As we went through the entrance I looked out to port to see what sort of a sea we would meet. It was a perfect specimen of an Atlantic swell rather higher than the bridge (50 feet) and it was breaking. The wheel was put hard over to swing the ship into the sea, and as the sea hit us I looked over the starboard side and saw the rocks close aboard. But the old ship came round beautifully and by the next time a sea hit us we were clear of the entrance. One felt serene and thankful after that!

'For eight solid hours we steered into the gale at eight knots but we only made twenty-four miles. Then we turned to run down past the Skelligs. This brought the sea just abaft the beam which meant considerable rolling yawing. As an instance of the latter, I happened to be watching the seas as they approached and noticed an outsize breaker which hit us on the starboard quarter. After we had taken this knock I looked at the compass to find that we had swung round 90 degrees as the result of the impact.

'Gradually the sea drew further astern and the motion eased a bit, but off the Fastnet we passed two large Atlantic liners which were lying hove-to with whom we exchanged signals—they had apparently suffered some damage from the heavy seas.

'Once around the Fastnet we were in the lee and cracked on for Queenstown, where after completing with fuel and landing our precious cargo, we were told to go to Portsmouth. This news filled everyone with joy. Without any delay off we went to our Home Port and leave. We were due for a full-power trial, so after consultation with the Chief, it was decided that we would do it on our way up Channel next morning. On getting round Land's End we ran into a nasty drizzle which brought visibility down to about a mile. But we had a following sea and worked up to full power. On the way up the Channel we did not sight any land, so when the dead reckoning showed that we should be about past St. Catherines in the Isle of Wight, I altered course for the Nab Tower and eased down to fifteen knots. Almost at once we sighted the Nab Tower right ahead. This filled me with satisfaction even more when, as the tide was right, the Commander-in-Chief Portsmouth gave us permission to proceed up harbour at once and go alongside the north-west wall in the Dockyard. This meant that the ship's company could start their Christmas leave at once.'

Although the Irish Civil War created special tasks for the destroyers of the 7th Flotilla, this month in the commission of H.M.S. *Wolsey* gives one a vivid idea of the valuable training destroyers gave to officers and men. The stresses of handling and navigating destroyers winkled out incompetents sooner than any other method yet devised. Practically all the future flag-officers of World War II went through the hard school of destroyer-command, and there were few who missed service in the 'Vs' and 'Ws'.

Between 1923 and 1925 there were a number of changes in the flotillas, which are best summarized as follows :

1923—3rd D.F. sent to Mediterranean (*Stuart* and 8 Modified 'Ws')
—4th D.F. sent to Mediterranean (*Montrose* and 8 Modified 'Ws')
—6th D.F. (Atlantic Fleet); *Shakespeare* relieved by *Valhalla*
—8th D.F. (reduced complements) *Bruce* and 8 'S' class
—9th D.F. (reduced complements); *Mackay* and 8 'V & W' class

1925—5th D.F. (Atl. Fl.) became 1st D.F. (Med.)
—2nd D.F. (Atl. Fl.) became 2nd D.F. (Med.)
—3rd D.F. joined by *Keppel* as leader on her first commission
—4th D.F. joined by *Broke* as leader on her first commission
—1st D.F. (Atl. Fl.) became 5th D.F.; *Wallace* and 8 'V & Ws'
—9th D.F. (reduced complements) became 7th D.F.
—8th D.F. (reduced complements) became 9th D.F.; *Shakespeare* and 8 'S' class

The 'V & W' classes now mustered their full strength, 65 boats and 12 leaders. They were the backbone of the Royal Navy's destroyer flotillas, with only 18 in reserve and 3 attached to the Torpedo Schools at Devonport and Portsmouth. The 1920s and 1930s were the heyday of the 'V & W' boats, with five flotillas in full commission. Despite the interludes of leave and fleet regattas it was a busy time for everyone from Captain (D) downwards, with endless drill and maintenance to be carried out. There was small-arms drill, gunnery practice, torpedo firing, anti-submarine exercises and a host of minor jobs to do. The Navy was experimenting with new ideas such as naval aviation, and destroyers had to be provided for co-operation with aircraft-carriers; the experience gained with submarines from 1914 to 1918 had not been thrown away, and strenuous efforts were made to use submarines in realistic exercises against surface warships; the first running destroyers fitted with the anti-submarine detection device ASDIC were 'V & W' boats of the 6th flotilla in 1923, although others received it in the course of refits as the years passed.

Destroyer tactics evolved steadily during the 1920s, and constant rehearsal improved on the practical knowledge learned during World War I. Massed attacks were much in vogue right through into the 1930s—refined versions of the destroyer-tactics of Jutland, with flotillas of destroyers in line approaching the 'enemy' battlefleet at approximately right angles to the firing course, all done at high speed and requiring seamanship of a high order. It has already been pointed out that the old large flotillas of sixteen destroyers were too large for effective control, and flotillas of eight (plus one leader) had been introduced in 1921. This problem was even more acute when night fighting was necessary, and it became clear from analysis of post-war exercises that the division or half-flotilla was a better unit for night attack. In fact this point had been made by Roger Keyes long before 1914, and seems to have been overlooked by the time Jutland was fought. With the 50 per cent increase in torpedo armament introduced in the 'V & W' classes the validity of divisional tactics was further strengthened.

In the 'V & W' classes torpedoes could be fired with the tubes on a relative bearing of 70°, 90° or 110°, or in other words, between 20° before and 20° abaft the beam. However, in practice the beam bearing was usually chosen to avoid the risk of the bridge sight being on a different bearing from the tubes. Torpedoes were aimed by swinging the ship to bring the sight on to the target. The Torpedo Control Officer would warn the Captain when the sight was 10° or 15° off, and the rudder would usually be eased to allow a slight time interval and small spread of angle between torpedoes. This was to reduce the risk of one torpedo colliding with another, or even counter-mining it. British destroyers had to wait until World War II for the refinement of torpedo gyros which permitted the torpedoes to be fired on the run-in and then swung on to the correct bearing, without waiting for the destroyer to swing round and present her broadside to enemy retaliation.

By the 1930s the 'V & W' boats were beginning to lag behind in some respects, notably their fire-control, which one C.O. described as a 'Harry Tate Transmitting Station with its rate clock and a chap with a stop-watch in one hand, hitting a drum with the other'. This had been good enough in 1917, but even before the advent of radar it was clear that improved fire-control would probably be decisive. Destroyers were still gun-armed vessels intended to sink and disable their opposite numbers before going on to sink the enemy fleet with torpedoes, and therefore they could not risk being outgunned by other destroyers. It was this doctrine carried to its logical conclusion which led to the building of the 'Tribal' class destroyers, in essence 'V & W' destroyers with twin 4·7-inch guns, but achieved at the expense of halving the torpedo armament. This was, in the writer's opinion, quite unjustified, as it clung to an outdated concept of the superiority of gun over torpedo. If anyone questions this, let him compare the 'Tribal' design with the *Javelin* type which followed it; by sacrificing a twin-gun mounting, room was found for *ten* torpedo-tubes instead of four.

# Chapter 4

# THE MED. AND CHINA STATIONS

THE first 'V & W' flotilla sent to the Mediterranean was the 3rd, eight 'Modified Ws' under the leader *Campbell*. When the war between Greece and Turkey ended in the disastrous Greek evacuation of Smyrna in 1922 the Mediterranean Fleet had to be hurriedly reinforced from the Atlantic Fleet. The 3rd Flotilla had the unenviable job of covering the evacuation of all Greek-held islands in the Sea of Marmora, to ensure that the Turks did not violate the peace treaty by molesting the Greeks during their flight.

The scene was invariably harrowing; at each island a transport would be found embarking Greek personnel, with the sea around the embarkation point covered with a hideous flotsam of slaughtered sheep, cattle and goats. All buildings were set on fire, and all livestock slaughtered, as the Greeks were only allowed a minimum of personal effects. Ironically, the plight of the men of the 3rd Flotilla was nearly as bad as that of the wretched Greek soldiery, for the destroyers had left England in such haste that they had been given no time to take on additional stores, and the ships' companies were desperately short of food. Parties were sent ashore to forage, but all that remained seemed to be onions or vegetables.

One evening the *Wild Swan*'s whaler was sent ashore to land a party at a small village. The landing-party found that the local wine-tavern's stocks were still intact, although sentenced to be destroyed that evening. To their chagrin the Captain forced them to forego a bacchanalian orgy, and the casks were duly smashed; although the streets ran with wine the mood was hardly festive.

As Christmas was near, all the ingredients for a Christmas 'duff' had to be scrounged from the big ships, but fortunately the destroyers were allowed to go to Mudros, where their depot-ship *Sandhurst* was able to make good all the deficiencies. Obviously the old messing system could not stand up to the conditions of prolonged absence on detached duty, and a canteen system would have solved most of the problems. The old system was devised when destroyers never operated far from their base, but after World War I destroyers grew large enough to operate at greater distances, and so their messing arrangements had to be adapted. When the 3rd Flotilla recommissioned for the Mediterranean in 1924 each ship was equiped with a canteen, situated in a space formerly used as a room for drying oilskins. The canteen was in the charge of a Maltese manager, who stocked up from the N.A.C.B. (forerunner of the N.A.A.F.I.), or went ashore to get fruit and vegetables locally if needed.

It is not surprising that the Mediterranean Fleet destroyers were by and large happy ships. The warm, sunny climate made for good health, and the intervals between exercises and routine duties were not too rare. Discipline is always less formal in small ships, and stories of the carefree days in the Med. are legion. As an example, when the 3rd Flotilla was cruising in the Greek islands and one of the ships was at anchor, the 1st Lieutenant would pass the word that anyone wishing to make up a 'banyan party' ashore would be allowed to use the whaler. At some shady spot on the beach everyone would relax over tea, while the more energetic souls might join the 1st Lieutenant in a game of water-polo.

The other recreation was training for the flotilla regatta; there were all sorts of events, Communications Dinghy, E.R.A.'s Dinghy, Stokers' Whaler, etc., and somebody was always training for one event or another. Flotilla regattas were followed by a Fleet regatta, and there was a similar series of boxing championships. Personal recreation took many forms; some messes organized a band, and the traditional games of 'Housey Housey' (at 2d. per card, by permission of the Captain) and 'Uckers' were always popular. The main burden on men's minds was their inevitable separation from wives and families, but apart from this, the cosy life in destroyers was congenial. To quote an ex-destroyer officer: 'Someone should describe the cosiness of those wardrooms. A winter night with the stove glowing; the Pusser's leather armchairs, with their back legs shortened; the shelf running right around the bulkheads and ship's sides, so that one could put one's gin glass down wherever one was; the little round "occasional" tables, with a brass cordite case serving as a pedestal and as an ashtray.' An ex-E.R.A. has similar memories of the messdecks on a Sunday morning in Malta : 'All the tin gear sparkling, the stools and tables scrubbed white, and the sun glittering through the scuttles.'

### 'Pozzuoli Sunday'

On 9 March 1932 the Mediterranean Fleet left Malta for the annual Spring Cruise. The destroyers attached were under the command of Rear-Admiral Frank Forester Rose, flying his flag in the light cruiser *Coventry*. 'Biff' Rose was a destroyer-man of many years' experience, and had been badly wounded in the Battle of Heligoland Bight in August 1914. His command was made up as follows :

**1st Flotilla:** *Mackay, Waterhen, Vendetta, Vampire, Vimiera, Wryneck, Walrus, Vivacious* and *Voyager*.

**2nd Flotilla:** *Stuart, Vanessa, Venetia, Viscount, Vanquisher, Valentine, Vega, Winchelsea* and *Viceroy*.

**3rd Flotilla:** *Active* (acting as Captain (D)'s ship), *Arrow, Acasta, Achates, Ardent, Worcester* and *Antelope* (the leader, *Codrington* was in dock).

**4th Flotilla:** *Keith, Basilisk, Bulldog, Boreas, Boadicea, Blanche, Beagle* and *Brilliant* (*Brazen* in dock).

As an economy measure the Combined Mediterranean and Home Fleet exercises were not to be held; instead the Mediterranean Fleet was to cruise independently in the Western Med., starting with a visit to Naples.

O.U.N.E. the destroyers were subjected to a rigorous programme of exercises, in order to extract the maximum benefit from the expenditure of fuel. In unpleasant weather the destroyers were put through their paces. R-A (D) singled out the unfortunate 1st Flotilla for most criticism; the ships had commissioned at the end of the previous year, and were not worked up to any pitch of efficiency. R-A (D)'s signals grew more waspish: 'Indicate the name of the Officer of the Watch'; 'Take up your appointed station'; 'The station-keeping of the flotillas generally leaves much to be desired';

'That of *Mackay* and *Wryneck* is disgraceful', etc., etc. As the exercise continued tempers shortened, and bodies grew weary. When Saturday 12 March dawned the clear sky was a welcome omen, for it meant that the exercises had to stop while the destroyers entered the Gulf of Naples.

The Mediterranean Fleet split up, and the destroyers were ordered to anchor in Pozzuoli Bay, in the north west corner of the Gulf. Disposed according to their order of berthing, and led by the *Coventry*, the three flotillas made their way into Pozzuoli Bay, but at about half-way they were obstructed by a flock of Neapolitan fishing-boats. As the Rule of the Road dictated that steam give way to sail R-A (D) had no choice but to order a Blue Pendant turn (16 points, or 180°). According to an eyewitness this process had to be repeated several times; since the procedure for moving twenty-five destroyers backwards and forwards at moderate speed is quite a lengthy one, it will be appeciated that the afternoon began to drag. Finally Admiral Rose abandoned the original proposal, and the destroyers anchored in succession, a less spectacular method, but in the circumstances a more practical one. Officers and men in the flotillas were exhausted, and so little was done to smarten up the ships before allowing everyone to get their heads down. In addition, the Invergordon mutiny was a fresh memory in the Navy, and all first lieutenants felt that it might be imprudent to insist on 'bull' after three days and nights of exercises. Again, thanks to the economy drive, the ration of paint had been cut, and it was not easy to find enough to restore the destroyers to their pristine glory.

Some of the destroyers did look in poor shape, having come out of Malta Dockyard only a few days before sailing. The *Vampire* had been used to test a new type of paint, and had strict orders from the Admiral Superintendent not to attempt any touching up, apart from a small tin left aboard for 'touching up scratches'. The paint was not a success, and the unfortunate *Vampire* looked dreadful. The *Vimiera* also had paint problems, for she had deferred her painting until the last day before sailing, and as it had rained heavily while the pendant numbers were being painted up on her bow and stern, the figures had streaks of black paint running down over the grey.

Next morning the storm broke. Admiral Rose went away from

his flagship in his barge to carry out the usual informal inspection, but instead of the expected signal listing the failings of individual ships, there was an order to C.O.s and 1st Lieutenants to repair on board *Coventry*. As it was Sunday the officers were in frock coats, and merely put on their swords before complying with the order. In some trepidation everyone lined up on the quarterdeck, the three Captains (D) made to stand by the quarterdeck screen, close to the door of the Admiral's cabin, the remaining C.O.s in two ranks fore and aft, and finally the 1st Lieutenants in three ranks amidships.

When Admiral Rose appeared he cleared the quarterdeck of gang-way staff, and proceeded to abuse the officers 'like pickpockets' as one of the delinquents later put it. In a towering rage he threatened to apply for wholesale reliefs for officers who allowed their ships to be a public disgrace. 'If you Commanding Officers cannot take the trouble to get into a boat and inspect the outside of your ships, then you will cease to be ... (followed by a sinister pause) ... Commanding Officers.' Then he turned on the 1st Lieutenants, and his wrath took a more personal turn, 'And as for you, young gentlemen, don't you ever wash your necks?' At this point a lieutenant in the rear rank smiled nervously, an unfortunate idiosyncrasy which drove Rose to new heights of frenzy. Convinced that he was being mocked, he seemed to be struck dumb by the enormity of the offence; although he turned on the officer, and might well have struck him, as he was by now almost black in the face with rage, he was unable to utter a word. In the dreadful silence that ensued the Admiral walked slowly and haltingly back to his cabin, and one by one the delinquents fell out and crept away.

The incident did not end there, for the officers had been dressed down in terms more appropriate to midshipmen, all in full view of their boat-crews. No doubt the consumption of gin in the wardrooms reached an all-time peak that night as the officers smarted under Rose's tongue-lashing, but as time went on 'Pozzuoli Sunday' was seen as nothing more than an embarrassing incident, the most devastating 'rocket' on record. Common sense and a tactful suggestion that Admiral Rose was suffering from toothache helped to put things in their proper perspective.

\*

The second disruption in the distribution of flotillas was caused by the civil war raging in China between the forces of Chiang-Kai-Shek and the Communists. After several demonstrations of hostility to foreigners all Europeans resident in China were advised to withdraw to the Floating Concessions at the various Treaty Ports, where they could be guarded with greater ease by warships. From 1922 to 1926 there had been no British destroyers on the China Station, under an agreement with the United States whereby the station was provided with British submarines and American destroyers. However, in the troubled atmosphere prevailing this agreement was quietly shelved, and the 3rd Flotilla was sent to China from the Mediterranean to reinforce the cruisers, submarines and gunboats already there. As we have seen, this flotilla was composed of the new leader *Keppel* and eight Modified 'W' class, the most modern destroyers in the Royal Navy.

Lieutenant Eric Bush (later Capt. Bush, D.S.O.**, D.S.C., R.N.) joined the *Veteran* at Hankow and described the experience:

'The *Veteran* lay alongside the *Negus* pontoon, off the Hankow bund and opposite the Hong Kong and Shanghai Bank. Secured to her port side and towering above her was Messrs. Butterfield & Swire's river steamer *Ngankin*, and on the shore side of the pontoon Messrs. Jardine, Matheson & Co.'s *Siangwo*. We were completely hemmed in. . . .

'Life in a destroyer under these conditions was something no one had ever experienced before. Except to move down river occasionally to another Treaty Port, where the same routine prevailed, we did no steaming at all for months on end. In fact, except to land on the pontoon or, on one or two rare occasions, venture as far as the bund, we never stepped off the *Veteran* for eight months, which must be a record for modern times. The other destroyers in our flotilla had a similar story to tell.' [1]

Landing parties were constantly required to protect property or to deal with parties of obstreperous Chinese soldiery trying to travel free on British river-steamers. Things had not changed much since the days of 'Chinese' Gordon, when the soldier's lowly status in the Chinese social order was reflected in his vicious habits; many of the

1. Quoted from *Bless Our Ship*, Allen & Unwin (1958).

worst outrages inflicted on Chinese civilians were the work of the very soldiers employed to protect them. A further complication was the tendency for both factions in the civil war to blame the foreigner for China's woes (not an unfair view, when all is considered), and Communists and Nationalists found common ground in baiting the foreigner.

With trouble continuing in China the *Bruce* and eight 'S' class destroyers were brought forward from reserve and sent out to form a permanent China Station flotilla (the 8th) and to relieve the Mediterranean flotilla. On 15 May 1928 the 3rd Flotilla left for home, with the band of the flagship playing 'Rolling Home' as each destroyer slipped past her out of Hong Kong. That tune was bitterly remembered as the flotilla battled against the south-west monsoon from Singapore to Colombo, and then on the 2,000-mile leg to Aden. Nine battered and weary destroyers limped into Aden with scarcely three days' fuel left.

At about this time the destroyers in Reserve were reorganized. In place of the two Atlantic Fleet flotillas, the 7th and 9th, with nine destroyers each in nominal commission with reduced crews, a Maintenance Reserve was set up at Chatham, Devonport and Rosyth. The basic idea was a sound one, to economize in manpower, in view of the financial stringency affecting all three Services. By having a care and maintenance party to look after a batch of destroyers by periodic inspections, and only enough ratings to provide reduced complements for a few, it could be possible to do enough essential repair work to keep all the destroyers in a reasonable state. The limitation of the scheme was that a small number of men could not carry out all the necessary repairs, and since in due course expenditure of money on reserve ships was cut even further the ships deteriorated. Destroyers are complex vessels which tend to decay in a hundred ways if not inspected and repaired from time to time; wiring corrodes, plating gets thinner and all the external fittings suffer from salt air (the luxury of plastic 'cocooning' did not exist in the 1930s, and one wonders whether the Navy could have spared the money for the older destroyers if it *had* been available).

In time the Maintenance Reserve was concentrated at Rosyth as a further measure of economy. It was felt that the older destroyers tended to become worn out by constant service (which was true), and the policy was to pay some of them off for a spell in Maintenance Reserve in order to extend their useful life.[1] But the penny-wise economies imposed by the Treasury on the Navy meant that the majority of the destroyers which went into the Maintenance Reserve emerged only to be towed to the breakers. One is tempted to claim that the years of arduous service by the 'V & W' boats from 1920 to 1935 actually *saved* them from the breakers' yard because essential running repairs were carried out to keep them going, the same essential maintenance which was denied to many ships in reserve. It should be remembered that the 'Vs' and 'Ws' were the most modern destroyers in the Fleet until 1930, when the new leader *Codrington* and the 'A' class replaced them in the 3rd Flotilla in the Mediterranean. The two experimental prototypes *Amazon* and *Ambuscade* (completed in 1926) had been engaged in lengthy trials, and did not become fully fledged fleet destroyers for some time.

In 1931 the 4th Flotilla of Modified 'Ws' were relieved by the new 'B' class, but a year later they went to China under the leader *Keppel*, which was enjoying her second tour of duty as Captain (D)'s ship on that station.

The London Treaty of 1930 had laid down a maximum age of fifteen years for destroyers, and if the clause stipulating that two years' war service were to count as one peacetime year was to be taken seriously, all the older 'V' and 'W' boats would have to be scrapped by 1932. In other words, the Royal Navy would lose over fifty destroyers, having added fewer than thirty. It was out of the question, particularly since no other naval power was inclined to scrap destroyers en masse, and so the veterans had to continue in service willy-nilly. As it turned out, only one 'V' class went to the scrapyard; she was the *Valhalla*, one of the oldest, sold in December 1931, just over fourteen years after entering service. In her case the decision may have been hastened by the fact that she needed extensive repairs after ten years' continuous service, and was considered unworthy of further expense.

In 1936 the old destroyers were victims of a deal which accounted for six of their number. The famous liner *Majestic* had been sold

1. See Adm 138/578, in which the D.N.C. makes this point.

for breaking up in May that year, but before the buyers could begin their melancholy work the Admiralty offered to buy her back in order to turn her into an artificer-cadets' training ship. Naturally the Admiralty was loath to pay hard cash, and offered to replace the *Majestic* with her equivalent tonnage in obsolete warships. Along with a number of other warships, including some 'S' class destroyers, the *Shakespeare, Spenser, Valkyrie, Vectis, Venturous* and *Violent* were sacrificed. They had spent eleven to fifteen years in the so-called Maintenance Reserve, and if they were beyond repair this seems to have been the cause. Within two years the international situation was to alter so much for the worse that the loss of even six of these fine vessels would be a matter for regret, but in 1936 another world war seemed far away.

When at last the rundown of the Royal Navy was halted in 1938, the desperate shortage of destroyers was one of the problems which worried the new First Sea Lord, Sir Roger Backhouse. Magnificent new destroyers were in hand, the famous 'Tribals', and the 'Js' and 'Ks', but they could still only be turned out in batches of eight each year, and they absorbed material and gun-mountings faster than Britain's wasted resources could produce them. Sir Andrew Cunningham as Deputy Chief of Naval Staff put forward a suggestion for building 'fast escort vessels' or utility destroyers which could be built faster and more cheaply. As these would not be ready until 1940 it was agreed that a simultaneous programme of modernizing the 'Vs' and 'Ws' would provide a stopgap, and so began the last act in the 'V & W' story. They had sunk a long way, from being the cream of the Navy's destroyers twenty years before to tired old workhorses, but now they were a vital element in the Admiralty's rearmament plans.

The proposed fast escort vessels, later known as the 'Hunt' class escort destroyers, were designed to escort the vulnerable East Coast convoys, and the proposed 'V & W' escort vessel was given a comparable armament of modern high-angle guns. Twenty were earmarked for conversion, to be known as the 'Wair' type, but almost immediately an additional destroyer had to be allocated, for on 13 February 1938, while en route from Rosyth to begin her refit at Chatham, the *Walrus* broke her tow and ran aground off Scarborough.

57

She was stripped of various fittings by a salvage team, but proved to be damaged beyond repair, and the hull was scrapped.

The 'Wair' conversion involved a lot of work, for rusted plating had to be renewed, defective boilers needed repair, and wiring had to be replaced, all basic renovation. The superstructure was removed entirely, for the 4-inch twin anti-aircraft mountings needed a fresh arrangement, one on the forecastle and the other sited aft on a larger deckhouse; this in turn involved new firing circuits and altered ammunition supply. The old flimsy bridge structure which had been adequate in 1917 was replaced by a new enclosed steel bridge of greater strength, which was also large enough to accommodate bridge personnel in relative comfort. Above the bridge was a modern fire-control system which in due course would benefit from the addition of R.D.F., later known as radar.

The critical shortages and delays in weapon-production which hindered British rearmament are well illustrated by the secondary armament of the 'Wairs'; this comprised nothing better than a pair of quadruple ·5-inch machine-guns, weapons which proved to be of dubious value as a close-range defence against aircraft. As production of 20-mm. Oerlikon guns increased they replaced the ·5-inch guns and were added in the bridge-wings, but in many ships the old weapons were still in place as late as 1943. The leader *Wallace*, being considerably larger than the 'V & W' boats, was given a somewhat heavier scale of armament. In addition to the 4-inch and ·5-inch mountings she had a four-barrelled pom-pom on the quarterdeck, which gave her a fighting chance against dive-bombers.[1]

When war broke out in September 1939 only three, *Wallace, Valorous* and *Whitley* were completed, with *Vivien, Vega* and *Woolston* almost complete. A further nine were completed (see Part II), the last, the *Viceroy* in January 1941; owing to the pressure on dockyard resources three were never taken in hand, and served as ordinary escort destroyers.

1. By sheer accident the pom-pom in the *Wallace* was sited more advantageously than the same weapon in the latest fleet destroyers; whereas theirs were amidships and masked by superstructure, the *Wallace*'s pom-pom fired aft, the angle from which German aircraft usually attacked.

# Chapter 5

# SERVICE IN WORLD WAR II

WHEN war broke out in September 1939 the distribution of the 'Vs' and 'Ws' and old leaders was as follows :

1. **11th Destroyer Flotilla,** Western Approaches Command
*Mackay, Vanquisher, Versatile, Vimy, Walker, Warwick, Whirlwind* and *Winchelsea,* with *Vanoc* to join.

2. **13th Destroyer Flotilla,** North Atlantic Command
*Douglas, Velox, Vidette, Watchman, Wishart* and *Wrestler* (four temporarily attached to Gibraltar Command).

3. **15th Destroyer Flotilla,** Rosyth
*Vanity, Vansittart, Volunteer, Wanderer, Whitehall, Witch, Witherington* and *Wolverine* (all eventually for transfer to Western Approaches Command).

4. **16th Destroyer Flotilla,** Portsmouth
*Malcolm, Venomous, Wivern, Wren* (to transfer to 18th).

5. **17th Destroyer Flotilla,** Western Approaches Command
*Keppel* (to transfer to 13th D.F.), *Vanessa, Viscount, Vivacious, Vortigen, Wakeful* and *Wessex. Windsor* (to transfer to 18th D.F.).

6. **18th Destroyer Flotilla,** Western Approaches Command
*Veteran, Whitshed* and *Wild Swan* (all to join on completion of refits).

7. **Rosyth Escort Force**
*Valorous, Wallace* and *Whitley* (+*Vega* ready to join).

8. **19th Destroyer Flotilla,** Nore Command
*Montrose.*

9. **4th Submarine Flotilla,** China
*Westcott* attached.

## 10. Royal Australian Navy

*Vampire, Vendetta* and *Voyager.*
*Stuart* and *Waterhen* in reserve at Sydney.

## 11. Escort Conversions in Hand

*Valentine, Verdun, Viceroy, Vimiera, Vivien, Westminster, Winchester, Wolfhound, Wolsey, Woolston* and *Wryneck.*

## 12. In Reserve

*Campbell, Venetia* and *Vesper* (commissioning for 17th D.F.).
*Walpole* and *Worcester.*

## 13. Target Service

*Bruce* (at Portsmouth).

Virtually all the old destroyers were either commissioning for service or completing refits, and only one, the unfortunate *Bruce*, was deprived of the chance to see service. She was expended as a target for the Navy's new 'Duplex' pistol for torpedo warheads. The Duplex, otherwise known as th 'C/N-C' or Contact/Non-Contact pistol was actuated magnetically to explode the torpedo *underneath* the target's hull; as its name implies it could also be set to explode as a simple contact pistol.

As preliminary trials had been satisfactory, the *Bruce* was attacked with a Fleet Air Arm 18-inch torpedo on 22 November 1939, off the Isle of Wight. The result was a devastating success (see pic. 22), and the old ship sank immediately. Unfortunately the Royal Navy's progress in this field was overshadowed by the introduction of degaussing, or neutralization of a ship's hull magnetism; when degaussing appeared the magnetic pistol's sensitivity had to be increased to a point where it could be influenced by the earth's magnetic field if the torpedo dived too deep. It was this phenomenon which was highlighted in May 1941 when the aerial torpedoes launched in error against the cruiser *Sheffield* during the *Bismarck* chase exploded prematurely. Fortunately, being Duplex pistols they could be reset to 'contact', and proved effective during the *Ark Royal*'s second strike against the *Bismarck*.

By early 1940 all excepting the 'Wairs' still converting were in commission, with thirty-one allocated to the vital Western Approaches

Command, eight at Gibraltar and the same number forming the Rosyth Escort Force. The Australian flotilla was in the East Indies, and the remaining few were scattered as far apart as Portsmouth and China. All the 'V & W' boats and leaders in Home Waters were escorting convoys and carrying out anti-submarine patrols, and on 30 January the *Whitshed* scored the first of the many submarine kills credited to the class. She shared her success with the sloop *Fowey* and aircraft of 228 Squadron, R.A.F., 100 miles West of Ushant; the victim was *U.55*.

Although it was quite clear before the war that the older 'V & W' destroyers were not fit for front-line service, the work they would have to do was still arduous. It was obvious that the messdecks would have to be adequately heated for winter patrols in the North Atlantic, and from 1938 various ships were taken in hand, beginning with the 'Wairs'. Apart from the provision of heating, bulkheads were lagged in order to insulate against the cold, but these overdue refinements had to wait until a destroyer came in for a major refit. With the entry of Russia into the war, and the institution of North Russian convoys, the old destroyers had to endure weather conditions worse than anything envisaged at the time they were built. To complicate matters the complement of all destroyers began to rise as the war progressed. New weapons and ancillary equipment required extra ratings and officers to operate them, and in the older destroyers the overcrowding on messdecks became very bad. Washing and sanitary facilities did not keep pace with the added numbers, and life became miserable after a few days of bad weather.

As a result of an investigation into living conditions aboard the old 'V & Ws' on escort duties, A.F.O.s 1394/40 and 959/41 laid down new standards of habitability, including electric heating, and lagging and lining of messdecks. In addition, the old 'hard-lying money', which had been abolished in the 1920s when canteen-messing came in, was re-introduced. It remained in effect from 1 October to 31 March each year, and lasted until 1945, for men serving in both the 'V & W' class and the equally venerable ex-American 'four-stackers', although connoisseurs claimed that a 'V & W' was always more comfortable than a 'four-stacker'.

The peacetime complement of a 'V & W' had been laid down as

110–15 officers and ratings before the war, but it rose to 131 by 1941 in those not converted. The following list of complements[1] shows the steep rise during wartime :

| | | |
|---|---|---|
| *Winchester* | (in 1940) | 125 |
| *Verdun* | (in 1940) | 134 |
| *Vanquisher* | (in 1941) | 132 |
| *Vanquisher* | (in 1943) | 167 |
| *Whitehall* | (in 1942) | 160 |
| *Vansittart* | (in 1942) | 169 |
| *Vanquisher* | (in 1944) | 170 |

By comparison, the peacetime complement of an old leader like the *Wallace* was 161, but this figure jumped to 187 in 1939, and must have risen even higher by 1944–5. The problem with destroyers was always the lack of space to accommodate extra personnel. Never roomy by civilian standards, destroyers even when built achieved miracles of compactness, and surplus space did not exist.

The chief drawback of the 'V & W' class as convoy escorts was lack of endurance, a fault which they shared with all the pre-war destroyers. No matter how many depth-charges could be stowed, an escort which could not stay with its convoy was ineffective. Although much was done to improve facilities for replenishment at sea, tanker-tonnage was itself so scarce that there was a limit to the number of tankers available to do this job. The problem with convoy escorts was the amount of steaming done in rounding up stragglers or investigating Asdic contacts; a destroyer might well find herself miles astern of the convoy, and would have to steam at full speed to catch up. In other words, the problem of endurance was not simply a matter of calculating the distance between Land's End and Halifax, Nova Scotia.

The short-term answer was to convert 'V & W' escorts by increasing their capacity. This involved removal of the forward boiler-room, and replacing it with a large fuel-tank. The first vessel to be modified was the *Vimy*, taken in hand at Portsmouth Dockyard in January 1941 for a six-month refit. When she reappeared her silhouette was distinctly odd, with only one short funnel well back from the fore-

1. From Cover Adm 138/578.

castle. Despite of the loss of a third of her boiler-power, she was still good for twenty-five knots, which would give her a good enough margin of speed for North Atlantic convoy work. The armament alterations followed the general pattern already described : reduction of the original armament and its replacement by close-range anti-aircraft guns and anti-submarine equipment.

In all nineteen destroyers of the 'V & W ' and 'Modified W' type were converted;[1] and the new type was known as the Long Range Escort; to distinguish the unconverted destroyers, these were subsequently designated Short Range Escorts. They included the older leaders (see above) and the second group of 'Modified W' boats, those with the thick forefunnel and thin afterfunnel. The reason for not converting the later 'Modified Ws' was their layout; it would have been impossible to put a fuel-tank between the forward double boiler-room and the engine-room. It was this factor which prevented any of the later 'A to I' classes from being similarly converted, for they had the same layout of boilers. The leaders had four boilers, as against three in the 'V & Ws', and it was probably felt that the loss of half the boiler-power would reduce speed too drastically.

Many of the Short Range Escorts went to the Mediterranean, or remained with the 'Wairs', covering East Coast convoys. On the Gibraltar run, or in the Mediterranean, short endurance did not prove such a handicap, but many of the unconverted destroyers such as the *Keppel,* rendered sterling service on the North Russian convoy route. *Keppel* established a record by participating in five U-boat 'kills'. Between September 1943 and September 1944 she helped to destroy *U.229, U344, U.360, U.394* and *U.713*. Others, such as the *Wrestler* and *Vidette*, sank three each.

The *Wolverine*'s most spectacular exploit was the ramming of the Italian submarine *Dagabur* during the course of the large convoy to Malta known as 'Pedestal', in May 1942. This was the convoy which included the famous tanker *Ohio*, and it proved to be crucial in enabling enough aircraft, fuel and ammunition to reach Malta. *Wolverine*

1. Although the leader *Keppel* is referred to in some sources as being converted to a long-range escort, I have been unable to verify this. No other leaders underwent this conversion, but her sister *Broke* had her fuel stowage altered in 1939–40.

was screening the carrier *Furious* while she flew off R.A.F. Spitfires for Malta, with the leaders *Keppel* and *Malcolm*. When *Wolverine* picked up a radar contact her captain ordered full speed. As she had been doing twenty-two knots the range closed rapidly, and she rammed the Italian submarine at approximately twenty-six knots, at the after end of the conning-tower. In a shower of sparks the old destroyer tore through the submarine's hull and came to a halt, surrounded by a pool of oil.

The *Wolverine* had sunk the *Dagabur* at the cost of considerable damage to herself, for her bows were badly crumpled and a steam pipe had burst in the engine-room. The 'bull ring' in the eyes of the ship was under water, and the forefoot of the stem had been driven up through the keel. Yet, despite the whole bow being folded downwards by the impact, the stempiece was undamaged.

\*

On 17 February 1945, *U.714*, a 770-ton Type VII.C U-boat, left Kiel after completion of her trials. Her commander, Kapitanleutnant Hans Joachim Schwebke, had orders to complete working up at Kristiansand and to patrol in an operational area off the East Coast of England, between the Firth of Forth and Flamborough Head. As *U.714* left Kristiansand on 4 March and was next heard of in the vicinity of Berwick ten days later, her movements are hard to account for. Whatever the reason for taking ten days to cross the North Sea to his patrol area, Schwebke sighted two merchantmen at about 1400 hours on Sunday 14 March; the two merchantmen were off Berwick, and their escort was a single 'Modified W' class destroyer. *U.714* hit and sank the second merchantman, the S.S. *Magne*, which had sailed with her consorts from Methil that morning to join a convoy assembling at Newcastle.

The escort, H.M.S. *Wivern*, immediately went into action, pausing only to drop her doctor into the water, to do what he could for the *Magne*'s survivors. This drastic step was justified by subsequent events, and the ship's doctor was apparently unharmed by his swim. An unexpected reinforcement materialized as the new South African frigate *Natal* appeared to seaward; she was a brand-new 'Loch' class

Two close-up views of the 'Modified W' class *Veteran* fitting out at Clyde-bank. Note the reversed thickness of funnels, the pom-poms lying shrouded between the funnels, and the greater size of the 4·7-inch guns. Seven were built to this layout, but another seven adhered to the standard 'V & W' funnel combination.

*Watchman* in the Bay of Biscay during the Home Fleet's Spring Cruise, 1934.

The two Thornycroft 'Modified Ws', *Wishart* (*above*) and *Witch* (*below*), were always held to be the handsomest of all, with two well-proportioned funnels and higher freeboard. Note that in common with all the 'V & W' boats between the wars, a range finder has been added on the bridge. *Wishart* is notable for having been under the command of Lord Louis Mountbatten.

*Walrus* high and dry at Scarborough in February 1938 after breaking her tow. Although she does not appear to be badly damaged from this photograph, she proved to be beyond economical repair, and the hull was subsequently stripped and broken up.

*Bruce* shown in her death agony as a torpedo explodes underneath her hull. Taken on November 22, 1939 off the Isle of Wight during tests of the 18-inch aerial torpedo fitted with a magnetic pistol.

Three views of one 'V & W', to show the alterations effected during the Second World War.

(1) (*Above*) *Velox* in 1940 with early additions to her anti-aircraft armament: a 12-pdr. gun in place of the second bank of torpedo tubes, two pompoms sited on platforms abaft the second funnel. Apart from these alterations, she remains much as she had been fifteen years before.

(2) (*Centre*) *c.* 1941–42 the *Velox* has had a Type 271 radar lantern added above the bridge as well as an air-warning aerial at the masthead. 'Y' gun on the quarterdeck has been replaced by enlarged depth charge stowage and throwers. The crow's nest was added early in the war in all 'V & W' boats.

(3) (*Below*) *Velox* in May 1944, after her curious conversion to a Long Range Escort. For some reason she never served in this role, despite the fact that No. 1 boiler has obviously been removed. In this photograph she is shown acting as a Flying Training Target, with deck stowage for twelve aerial torpedoes, as well as enlarged davits for recovering them. No anti-submarine gear is in evidence, and the close-range armament comprises four 20-mm Oerlikon guns.

Three views of the survivors of the *Scott* and *Shakespeare* classes:

(1) (*Above*) *Broke* as a Short Range Escort in 1942; she has the new 'Hedgehog' spigot mortar in place of 'A' gun, and the usual depth-charge gear in place of 'Y' gun, but the photograph shows that her forecastle has been extended aft, and the forefunnel totally altered from its original thickness. As a unit of the *Shakespeare* class, both funnels were equal in height, and flat-sided in the Thornycroft tradition. All the older destroyers with tall second funnels had them shortened during the war in order to improve arcs of fire for 20-mm guns in the bridge-wings.

(2) (*Centre*) *Montrose*, taken in 1944 after 'A' 4·7-inch gun had been re-placed by the big twin 6-pdr. weapon for use against E-boats. Unlike so many old destroyers, she has not had 'Y' removed from the quarterdeck, and a 4-inch anti-aircraft gun has replaced 'X' gun.

(3) (*Below*) *Douglas* shown in September 1942, with a 'Hedgehog' forward, and 'Huff-duff' mast against the after superstructure. The 12-pdr. anti-aircraft gun is in the same position as the pre-war 3-inch, and pom-pom positions have replaced the 4·7-inch gun between the funnels, as in *Montrose*.

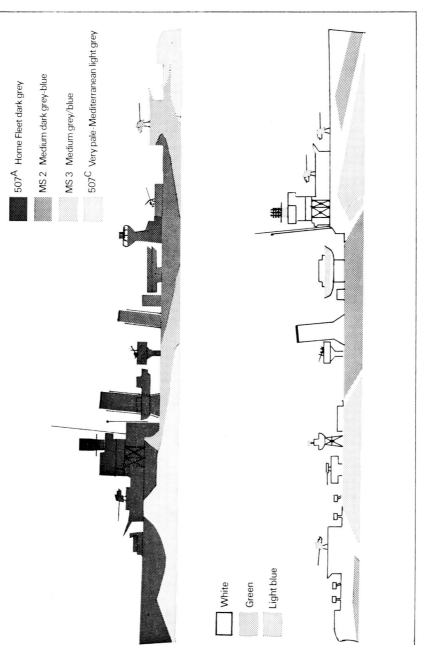

507<sup>A</sup>  Home Fleet dark grey

MS 2   Medium dark grey-blue

MS 3   Medium grey/blue

507<sup>C</sup>  Very pale - Mediterranean light grey

White

Green

Light blue

(*Above*) *Wolverine* with slight modification to Admiralty dark type 1942 camouflage.
(*Below*) *Whitehall* with standard 3-colour 1942 type Western Approaches camouflage.

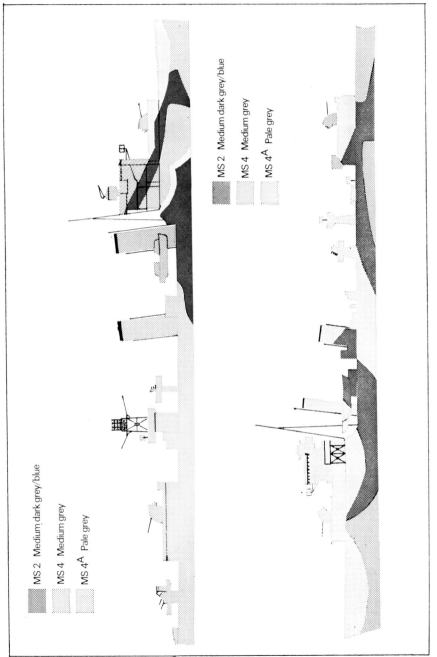

MS 2 Medium dark grey/blue

MS 4 Medium grey

MS 4<sup>A</sup> Pale grey

MS 2 Medium dark grey/blue

MS 4 Medium grey

MS 4<sup>A</sup> Pale grey

(*Above*) *Wallace* as in 1942 with 1942 type Admiralty light disruptive camouflage.
(*Below*) *Verdun* with slight modification to Admiralty light type camouflage.

(*Above and left*) *Viscount* was a sister of *Viceroy*, but instead of becoming a 'Wair' she became a Long Range Escort, having one funnel and boiler removed to allow for more oil fuel. In armament details she differed very little from the Short Range Escorts. On October 16, 1942 she rammed and sank *U.619* in the North Atlantic, sustaining only minor damage herself.

frigate, fitted with the latest radar and anti-submarine weapons, and was on passage to Scapa Flow to complete her working up.

*Wivern*'s C.O. called up *Natal* on T.B.S., and suggested that the South African ship should search to seaward, while the *Wivern* searched inshore from the point where the *Magne* had gone down. U-boats had been known to try the trick of hiding *inshore*, leaving the escorts to hunt fruitlessly to seaward, under the impression that their prey had made his escape.

Suddenly *Natal* picked up an Asdic contact, and fired two salvoes from her 'Squid' depth-charge mortars, six charges in all. At this point the South African C.O. announced that he was breaking off the action, on the grounds that he would be late for his working up at Scapa Flow. The time was now 1500, and the U-boat had vanished.

Left to continue the action alone, *Wivern* continued the search for some five hours, until she found an oil slick ten miles away. This proved to be from a submarine, which was in fact *U.714*, which was then attacked with depth-charges and destroyed. Two days later a special escort group from Scapa verified that the U-boat had not moved, and the wreck was blown open to make sure.

A question that remains to be answered is, why was *Wivern* not credited with the 'kill' in official Admiralty records? The *War at Sea* shows that *U.714* was sunk in the same place, on the same date, but by 'S.A.N.F. *Natal* on passage'. However, *Wivern*'s company was awarded three Mentions in Despatches for an action at which she was officially not present. Presumably it was felt at the time that the Royal Navy had so many U-boat kills to its credit that it could spare one for a fledgling Dominion navy, but the award of two D.S.C.s, two D.S.M.s, and five Mentions in Despatches to *Natal* seems a disproportionate share of the honours due for what must at most have been a shared kill.

Another 'V & W' operating on the East Coast was the 'Wair' *Viceroy*. The last sinkings of U-boats by surface ships in the European theatre took place in April 1945, and it is only fitting that a 'V & W' should be able to claim one of these. While escorting a southbound convoy on 16 April 1945 she successfully depth-charged *U.1274* off St. Abbs Head. Although the *Viceroy*'s captain (Lieutenant-

Commander Manners) was sure of his claim, there was no time to collect evidence, and he rejoined his convoy.

On her return to Rosyth with the next northbound convoy *Viceroy* was allowed to investigate the sinking, under the eagle eye of Captain (D), Rosyth Escort Force. The U-boat was duly located and depth-charged; this brought up some grisly souvenirs, but in addition an enormous cylindrical object shot to the surface. When brought alongside it proved to be six feet in diameter, and six feet long, with watertight clips and large hinges. In some trepidation the clips were taken off, and the contents were revealed—a splendid array of wines and spirits, packed in straw. Incredible though it may seem, the depth-charging had wrenched the cylinder free from its welded supports in the U-boat, without damaging any of the contents!

In view of the unique nature of the find, a casket was made in Rosyth Dockyard, and a selection of vintages was presented to the Prime Minister. Regrettably, after the remainder of the bottles had been distributed among the *Viceroy*'s crew, several members of the crew were charged duty on imported liquor; presumably there was insufficient evidence for trying them on charges of trading with the enemy.

*

It was by no means uncommon for a destroyer to ram a U-boat, but on one occasion at least, the tables were turned. In September 1942 a cornered U-boat turned on her pursuer and managed to inflict considerable damage before being sunk.

The *Vimy* was proceeding in company with two modern destroyers, *Quentin* and *Pathfinder* east of Trinidad, after handing over the damaged battleship *Queen Elizabeth* to an American escort, when a torpedo passed close by the *Quentin*. Asdic contact was quickly established, and all three ships dropped depth-charges, but after some hours the search was suspended; the *Vimy* was low on fuel, and it was hoped that a lull might tempt the U-boat to the surface.

*Vimy* zig-zagged to the north-west, heading for Trinidad at reduced speed, and hoping to pick up another contact. Within fifteen minutes a radar contact was picked up, about 3,000 yards away on the port bow. The officer of the watch sounded 'action stations' and

ordered speed to be increased, as the U-boat was now in view. As the
*Vimy* approached the U-boat, making twenty-three knots by this
time, the German fired two red flares at her bridge, which effectively
blinded everyone. Too late it was seen that the U-boat was going to
ram the *Vimy* aft, and when the order to reverse engines was given,
the *Vimy* was rolling so much that the seamen on the telegraphs were
both thrown to the deck.

The U-boat rammed *Vimy* in the forward boiler-room at a fine
angle, and the hydroplane cut into her plating above the waterline.
The U-boat lay bumping and grinding alongside, apparently immune
to anything the *Vimy* might try to do to her. But the *Vimy*'s captain
decided to risk firing a depth-charge, and ordered one of the port
depth-charge throwers to be set to fifty feet; *Vimy* went ahead
slowly as the charge was fired, which minimized the shock. The U-
boat took most of the blast, and rolled over and sank immediately,
leaving forty-nine survivors in the water.

Fortunately the U-boat (*U.162*) had collided at the point of the
fan bracket, one of the strongest points in the hull, and the plating
had not been pierced underwater, but the port propeller had been
seriously damaged. The *Vimy* had to be escorted by the corvette
*Burdock* to Gibraltar for repairs. *En route* she spotted what appeared
to be a conning-tower, and opened fire. As she drew closer the 'U-
boat' turned out to be a raft packed with survivors from an American
merchantman. As the *Vimy*'s damaged port propeller was causing a
great deal of vibration, and as her radar was out of action she had not
made good practice, but one of her 4-inch shells had carried away
the raft's sail! The Americans bore no illwill for the near-tragic
error, as nobody had been hurt, but the shock to the *Vimy*'s crew
must have been great.[1]

*

As we have seen, the wartime role assigned to the 'V & W' destroyers was definitely a subsidiary one, as they were no longer adequate to serve as fleet destroyers. Their hand-worked guns and
torpedo-tubes made it unlikely that they could participate effectively

1. From an article describing the incident in *The Navy*, November 1956, by
Commander H. G. D. de Chair, D.S.C.*, R.N. (Retd.).

with more modern destroyers against well-trained opponents. The record of the Australian destroyers in the Mediterranean showed that this was not strictly true, but there was another occasion when the 'V & Ws' had to take on some of the most up-to-date ships afloat, with no support from their own side, when five elderly destroyers carried out a 'forlorn hope' attack in daylight against the *Scharnhorst* and *Gneisenau*.

On 12 February 1942 the two German battle-cruisers carried out the most audacious plan of the war, a daylight dash up the Channel from Brest to their German bases, past a series of British defences designed to prevent that very event. Aircraft attacked, coastal guns thundered, and M.T.B.s threw themselves into the battle piecemeal, and all failed to stop the Germans, surrounded by escorting destroyers and torpedo boats, and covered by an umbrella of aircraft.

As the day wore on, and all the attacks came to nothing, orders were given to Captain (D), 21st Destroyer Flotilla at Harwich to attack with torpedoes. Captain C. T. M. Pizey, D.S.O. (later Admiral Sir Mark Pizey), was in the leader *Campbell*, and had only one other destroyer, the *Vivacious* in his flotilla; even with the *Mackay*, *Whitshed*, *Worcester* and *Walpole* of the 16th Flotilla to add to his command, there were still only six destroyers against two 32,000-ton battle-cruisers, one heavy cruiser, six large modern destroyers and fifteen torpedo boats, as well as E-boats and aircraft.

The plans for using the Harwich destroyers against the German ships had been drawn up by Vice-Admiral Ramsay in consultation with Captain Pizey, and it relied on the premise that the Germans, if they ever did manage to break out from Brest, would be forced to do so at night. Thanks to Hitler's intuition, the Germans gambled on the British being caught napping by a daylight dash, and as we know, they were right. All the piecemeal attacks might have had some chance of success at night, but the plans had never been modified to allow for daylight attacks.

The two flotillas were exercising off Harwich at 11.45 when the signal was received from Dover, 'Enemy battle-cruisers passing Boulogne speed about twenty knots. Proceed in execution of previous orders.' By chance the destroyers had been at fifteen minutes' readiness for steam; this had been reduced to four hours' readiness

68

after daybreak, but as the ships were already at sea Captain (D) was able to move off immediately. The ships were formed into two divisions, *Campbell, Vivacious* and *Worcester* in the First, and *Mackay* leading *Whitshed* and *Walpole* in the Second, and twenty-eight knots was ordered. Captain Pizey did not hesitate to take his two divisions through British minefields in order to reduce the time taken to reach a point of interception. The risk proved to be justified as the mines had been cleared a few days previously, but shortly after 1300 the *Walpole* ran her main bearings, and had to return to harbour; the forlorn hope had dropped from six ships to five. Shortly afterwards the first exchange of fire began, when two flights of German bombers attacked the *Mackay* out of low cloud; the bombs missed, and the destroyers continued to pound on towards their rendezvous. What followed next is somehow typical of the bungling and failure of inter-Service liaison which affected everything done that day : a British Hampden bomber carried out determined but ineffectual attacks on *Mackay* and *Worcester*, which the sailors bore with grim patience, foregoing the temptation to open fire.

At 1517 the enemy heavy ships were spotted on *Campbell's* radar, and as the first attack by Coastal Command Beauforts was in progress, the Germans were rudely surprised to see the First Division weeping aside the screen of E-boats as they rushed out of the mist with guns blazing. The German heavy units opened fire, and their official report claimed one British destroyer as sunk. However, Pizey's division had achieved something that had been considered impossible, in closing to 3,300 yards, firing torpedoes and escaping destruction. The destroyer which they thought they had sunk was the *Worcester*, which received the full weight of broadsides from the *Gneisenau* and the *Prinz Eugen*. By any normal standards of comparison the *Worcester* should have been sunk, for she was pounded at less than 4,000 yards by 11-inch and 8-inch salvoes, and at one stage, Lieutenant-Commander Coates ordered the ship's company to prepare to abandon ship. His ship was on fire, dead and wounded lay around the gun-positions, and scalding steam was pouring out of the engine-room. Unable to steam or to fight, the *Worcester* was in a sinking state as the Germans swept by, oblivious of anything that might delay their dash to safety.

Very few destroyers have ever survived the scale of punishment absorbed by the *Worcester*, and Captain Pizey was astounded when he returned to find the crippled destroyer valiantly tackling her fires and trying to raise steam. To add to their problems the ships were attacked repeatedly by German and British aircraft. But the R.A.F. proved no better at sinking British ships than they had at sinking Germans, and the four sound destroyers fussed around the *Worcester* as she limped home at eight knots. When she finally crawled into Harwich she gamely refused the aid of tugs and berthed herself unaided. Her casualties totalled seventeen dead and forty-five wounded, nearly half of her total complement of 130.

# Chapter 6

# DUNKIRK AND THE FALL
# OF FRANCE

'WARS are not won by evacuations,' said Winston Churchill of 'Operation Dynamo', but the evacuation of 338,000 soldiers from France effectively robbed the German Army of the victory it had won, and preserved the nucleus of the forces which returned via Normandy four years later. In 1940, however, the evacuation of the bulk of the British Expeditionary Force without weapons or vehicles was hard to see as a stepping-stone to D-Day. The speed of the German advance through the Low Countries and France increased the sense of catastrophe; the first German forces crossed into Holland on 10 May 1940, and the last British ship left Dunkirk exactly twenty-five days later. In less than a month one of the foremost military powers had virtually ceased to exist, and her partner's effective army had been reduced to one division. Fortunately, that partner's navy had not been overwhelmed, and stood firm as the first line of defence.

As early as October 1939 the possible need to block Dutch and Belgian ports had been foreseen, and the Royal Navy had made plans for the Nore Command to receive the necessary reinforcements. In 1914 the failure to block Ostende and Zeebrugge had given the U-boats a secure base for operations, and the Admiralty was determined to prevent this happening a second time. Four destroyers left Dover for Antwerp on 10 May, carrying demolition parties, and by the evening of 16 May the oil fuel tanks had been destroyed, the locks and basins had been blocked, and all shipping had been got clear. The only loss was the newly completed 'Wair' *Valentine*; she was sunk on 15 May while trying to protect the Scheldt ferries from German dive-bombers. In addition her sisters *Winchester* and *Westminster* were both badly damaged. *Westminster* was too badly crippled to reach an English port, but managed to limp to Dunkirk; not until 19 May was it possible to arrange for a rescue tug to tow her back. On that day, the next 'V & W' was sunk; the *Whitley* was operating under French orders north of Dunkirk, and had to be beached after heavy damage from Stukas. Four destroyers, all brand-new 'Wairs', were either sunk or out of action for some time.

The first hint of disaster was on 20 May, when Vice-Admiral Ramsay called a conference to discuss the possibility of the Navy evacuating large numbers of troops from France. The German forces were advancing across France, and had driven a wedge between the B.E.F. and the French. As the situation deteriorated hour by hour Lord Gort, the British C.-in-C., became more and more dominated by the need to fall back on a suitable embarkation point, preferably a port with adequate facilities to bring ships alongside. Three French ports, Dunkirk, Calais and Boulogne, were nominated, and a provisional figure of 10,000 men per day per port was fixed. Sixteen passenger steamers were held in readiness, and work began on the job of collecting smaller vessels. As the old Dynamo Room was chosen to accommodate the planning staff for this mammoth task, the code name for the evacuation of France became 'Dynamo'.

On 22 May the destroyers *Vimiera* and *Whitshed* escorted the 20th Guards Brigade to Boulogne, in order to secure the port against a thrust by the 2nd Panzer Division. When they arrived they found the quays littered with abandoned cars and equipment, but after heroic exertions order was restored in time to evacuate a large number of wounded, refugees and stragglers. The next day the Germans attacked in strength, but the perimeter hastily established by the Guards seemed to be holding, and the destroyers *Keith*, *Vimy* and *Wild Swan* were able to intervene by firing at 'targets of opportunity', tanks, artillery and motorized formations. The *Whitshed* accompanied other destroyers in covering the passage of the Rifle Brigade to Calais, and as soon as this had been completed she received orders to reinforce Boulogne. As she entered the harbour with H.M.S. *Keith* she came under fire from German machine-guns; while embarking stretcher-cases from the quayside, she engaged the enemy machine-gun posts with her 4·7-inch guns at little more than a hundred yards.

As she withdrew to allow the *Vimy* alongside, she fired some parting shots at Fort de la Crèche (now in German hands), and had the satisfaction of seeing a large explosion.

The situation at Boulogne had become so bad by late afternoon that a signal was sent to the destroyers to begin evacuation immediately. Although *Whitshed* had left for Dover to land her cargo of wounded men, three more 'V & Ws' arrived to replace her, the *Venetia, Vimiera* and *Venomous. Whitshed* later returned to help her sisters in evacuating the defenders, and had to repeat her performance of engaging machine-gun posts with her main armament. She and the *Vimiera* took over 1,000 men between them. When *Venetia* moved in at dusk between the breakwaters she came under heavy artillery fire, probably intended to sink her in the harbour entrance to block the evacuation. 'B' gun's crew was wiped out by a direct hit, and her captain and the entire bridge complement were severely wounded, with the result that she ran aground; fortunately Sub-Lieutenant Jones took command and got the destroyer out of her predicament. As she left stern first, the *Wild Swan*, already lying alongside the quay, spotted enemy tanks entering the town. One bold panzer commander had decided to reconnoitre a side street leading to the quayside, but he was stopped by a direct hit. Similarly, when *Venomous* came alongside she sighted a German motor-cycle detachment fanning out across the quay, opened up with both 2-pounder pom-poms, and broke up the column in some confusion.

The *Windsor* was ordered to leave Calais, and arrived at about 2230; she was able to pick up some 600 men. The last two undamaged destroyers of the Dover Command, the *Vimiera* and *Wessex*, were also ordered to help, but as *Wessex* was diverted to Calais, the *Vimiera* arrived at Boulogne alone, to find the port apparently deserted. After creeping alongside the outer jetty she waited in absolute silence for some time; with every nerve strained, officers and men called out, but there was no answer.

Finally the order was given to slip, but this was the signal for a sudden rush of refugees and French and Belgian soldiers who seem to have been hiding nearby. With them was a Guards officer who told *Vimiera*'s captain that a thousand men remained. By 2.45 the destroyer had taken 1,400 men on board, with every single inch of space excepting the gun-platforms occupied, and she was able to clear the harbour as it came under heavy shellfire and air attack. She was the last British ship to leave Boulogne, and any further resistance was limited to pockets of French soldiers making a last-ditch stand outside the town.

Only Calais and Dunkirk remained in British hands, and hope for the defenders of Calais was slender. Throughout 23 May destroyers carried out bombardments in support of the garrison, despite heavy air attacks which sank the *Wessex* and damaged the *Vimiera* and the Polish destroyer *Burza*. As the remaining ships were running out of ammunition the *Wolfhound* and *Verity* arrived from Dover with replenishments. Admiral Ramsay and his staff had hopes of evacuating the majority of the defenders, but the Chief of the Imperial General Staff sent a message independently to the Calais garrison advising them that evacuation would be impossible; the Navy continued to make its preparations in ignorance of this. On the night of 25 May a force of small ships was sent over to wait off Calais, and although some small vessels crept in and out with their cargoes of wounded soldiers, the orders never came through, and the Calais garrison fought on until the next day without relief. A brigade had been sacrificed to make Dunkirk safe for 'Dynamo'.

\*

On Sunday 26 May, at 1857, 'Operation Dynamo' began : thirty-five personnel ships (mainly cross-Channel steamers), forty Dutch 'schuyts' and a variety of barges and coasters, etc., had been mustered. But at this stage, the use of destroyers was not considered, and they were all retained on escort and bombardment duties. The front held by the B.E.F. was shrinking rapidly, but it had not yet reached the last perimeter, and the state of the battle was still fluid. Not until the surrender of the Belgians on 27 May did it become imperative to throw in every available ship, which Ramsay did in the late afternoon of that day. The patrolling destroyers were sent in, with the 'Wair' *Wolfhound* to act as communications ship off Dunkirk. To enable her to carry out this vital task the *Wolfhound* was given a special quota of communications staff under Captain W. G. Tennant.[1]

On 28 May the *Mackay, Montrose, Verity, Worcester, Sabre* and *Anthony* were sent in, and when it was clear that the battered moles in Dunkirk harbour were still usuable, the personnel ships were told to do likewise. Later the destroyers *Codrington, Gallant, Grenade, Jaguar, Javelin, Harvester, Malcolm, Esk, Express, Shikari* and *Scimitar* arrived, and the total of men evacuated began to rise dramatically. *Codrington* lifted 700 men on her first trip, and 900 on her second; with their good manoeuvrability and high speed the destroyers were able to cut the 'turn round' time dramatically, despite the fact that the shallow water restricted their speed to twenty-two knots during most of the passage. In the twenty-four hours ending at midnight on 28 May, 17,804 men reached England safely, and Ramsay and his staff became more sanguine about their chances of getting the main body of the B.E.F. away.

The toll was high, for the *Windsor* and *Wolsey* were both damaged. Next day was the worst from the destroyers' point of view, for two ships were lost. The *Wakeful* had made several trips, and early on the morning of 29 May she was heading for Dover in company with the *Grafton*, via the Zuydecoote Pass. Shortly before 1 a.m. while zigzagging at twenty knots, two torpedo-tracks were seen, just before one torpedo hit *Wakeful* amidships. The old destroyer broke in two and sank in fifteen seconds; only a few of her crew survived, and as most of the troops were between decks they had no chance of survival. The drifter *Nautilus* and the dan-layer *Comfort* came up, and helped the *Grafton* and the minesweeper *Lydd* to search for survivors, but no sooner had Commander Fisher of the *Wakeful* tried to warn the *Grafton* of her danger (he had been rescued by the *Comfort*), than she was hit by two more torpedoes. The enemy craft responsible was most probably the *Schnellboot S.30*, although a U-boat was also blamed at the time.

The sequel was grim, for the *Comfort* had circled out of sight, and as soon as she reappeared the sinking *Grafton* and the *Lydd* mistook

1. Chief Staff Officer to the First Sea Lord, Tennant had just been appointed to the battlecruiser *Repulse*, but volunteered to help with the evacuation; he subsequently took up his appointment, and survived when *Repulse* was sunk by the Japanese in 1941.

her for an E-boat. Most of her crew and troops were killed at short range by a hail of fire, with most of the *Wakeful* survivors, and then the *Lydd* rammed her at full speed.

The *Grafton* was torpedoed twice, and the torpedo which hit under the wardroom killed thirty-five Army officers sleeping there. The E-boat then machine-gunned the bridge and killed the captain before disappearing into the darkness. Most of the survivors were removed, but the twin tragedy must have accounted for the loss of over 1,000 lives. The shallow waters around Dunkirk were ideal for attacks by E-boats, and it is surprising that similar tragedies did not occur throughout the nine days of Dunkirk.

The *Montrose* had her bows blown off, and lay helpless under the glare of German searchlights at Cap Gris Nez before being towed away by tugs. The *Intrepid* and *Saladin* were damaged, and many ships reported heavy air attacks during the passage. The *Grenade* was set on fire in the roadstead, and drifted about the fairway, living up to her name as her ammunition continued to explode. In addition to the hazards of bombs and mines, the ships had to run the gauntlet of German guns north and south of Dunkirk, as the navigable channels hugged the coast for some way out.

On Thursday 30 May the destroyers set new records as they lifted more troops than ever. The *Sabre* brought 1,700 men back to Dover in two trips; *Wolsey* lifted 1,677 in three trips; *Vimy, Vanquisher, Vivacious, Whitehall* and *Express* all lifted over a thousand men each. In addition to this phenomenal achievement, the destroyers also bore the brunt of patrol work. A screen was maintained to keep E-boats away, in order to avoid another *Wakeful* and *Grafton* disaster, and anti-submarine patrols had to be extended. Both flanks of the Dunkirk perimeter were also watched, and the destroyers carried out intermittent counter-battery work. Seen against this, the exertions of the destroyers off the beaches are even more remarkable, and one can only wonder at the strain imposed on men and ships.

The story continues to 1 June, when the Germans timed a ferocious air-attack on shipping to coincide with an assault on the land-perimeter. The air-attack hit the destroyers *Keith, Ivanhoe, Basilisk* and *Worcester*, of which only *Ivanhoe* and *Worcester* survived to limp home. The fury of this attack would have been disastrous to

'Operation Dynamo' if it had been mounted earlier, but fortunately the harbour was not blocked by any of the ships sunk by bombs, and the evacuation continued until 23.30 on Sunday 2 June, when Captain Tennant sent the final signal, 'B.E.F. evacuated'.

Only one job remained undone, the evacuation of the rearguard. Although there were only a few British beach parties still ashore, an estimated 30,000 French soldiers were still holding out, and Admiral Ramsay was determined to make an effort to get them away on the night of 3 June. The destroyers again played a vital role, and despite the sudden appearance of 40,000 French stragglers and a total breakdown of beach organization, 26,000 men were evacuated. Unfortunately the unforeseen arrival of 40,000 unarmed French troops who appear to have remained in hiding throughout the evacuation, made it all but impossible to evacuate the gallant fighting rearguard under General Bathélémy. The men who held the last of the Dunkirk perimeter had to watch their places in the ships taken by men who had done nothing to aid the defence.

Despite the frustration of Ramsay's plans for the last two nights of 'Dynamo', the preceding week had achieved the miracle of retrieving the B.E.F. Out of thirty-eight British destroyers involved in 'Operation Dynamo' sixteen were 'V & Ws' or old leaders.[1] One was sunk and six were damaged. After Dunkirk, the Royal Navy had only seventy-four destroyers undamaged, which shows clearly how vital the 'V & W' destroyers were to British survival. If the fifty American destroyers were essential to make good the losses, how much more crucial might the shortage have been if the 'V & W' destroyers had been written off in the 1930s? Had the older 'V & W' boats not existed in 1940, the shortage would have been greater, the evacuation might have suffered, and worst of all, the Navy might have been unable to find enough destroyers to cope with Hitler's planned invasion.

There is something appropriate in the way that the old destroyers gave of their utmost in the hour of crisis. Having missed the opportunity of distinguishing themselves in a previous war they more than

1. *Mackay, Malcolm, Montrose, Vanquisher, Venomous, Verity, Vimy, Vivacious, Wakeful, Whitehall, Whitshed, Winchelsea, Windsor, Wolfhound, Wolsey* and *Worcester.*

made up for this by their efforts in 1940, like veterans recalled to the colours. The 'V & W' destroyers can count Dunkirk as their finest hour; for all their work in the Battle of the Atlantic, nothing can compare with their labours in May and June 1940. In nine days they did more fighting and steaming than they had throughout their lives, and their aged hulls were equal to the challenge.

# Chapter 7

# THE SAGA OF THE SCRAP-IRON FLOTILLA

I F any five destroyers could be singled out as the best examples of 'V & W' tenacity and longevity, they would be the *Stuart, Vampire, Vendetta, Voyager* and *Waterhen*. These five ships won legendary fame in their own lifetime by their exploits in World War II, and fought from Gibraltar to Singapore under the Australian ensign; in their honour four of the names have been revived for the post-war R.A.N. (the fifth, *Waterhen* was cancelled).

In 1932 the Australian Navy Board began negotiations with the Admiralty to acquire a new destroyer-force to replace the ageing *Anzac* and 'S' class destroyers. After a certain amount of considera-tion, the leader *Stuart,*[1] then attached to the 2nd Submarine Flotilla in the Home Fleet, and a division of the 3rd Flotilla, Mediterranean Fleet were chosen. After a refit, the new force left for Australia on 17 October 1933 under Captain A. G. Lilley, R.N. During the next six years the *Stuart* remained in commission as Captain (D)'s ship at Sydney, while the others played Box & Cox in and out of reserve.

After a brief spell in the East Indies after the outbreak of war, all five were offered to the Admiralty for use in the Mediterranean, as it was obvious that the shortage of British ships in that theatre was a standing temptation to Mussolini to intervene. The Admiralty ac-cepted the offer with alacrity, and the Australian destroyers became the 10th Flotilla (19th Division). Their new Captain (D) was a man whose reputation was to become an inspiration to the whole Aus-tralian Navy, the immortal 'Hec' Waller.

Captain Waller's destroyers soon showed their mettle; hostilities

1. See Adm 138/380 for discussions on the choice of leader; *Mackay* and *Montrose* were also considered.

against Italy began on 10 June 1940, and within four days both *Stuart* and *Voyager* had attacked Italian submarines. Although it was thought at the time that the attacks had been successful, the claims were not substantiated. Earlier, Waller gave a superb demonstration of seamanship by saving the crippled tanker *Trocas* from certain loss off Tripoli. *Stuart* was able to get alongside the tanker before she drifted on to a lee shore, and towed her back to Malta despite thick fog.

Before the end of June 1940 the *Stuart* was in action at Bardia, supporting a bombardment of shore positions by the French battleship *Lorraine* and the cruiser H.M.A.S. *Sydney*. The following months were a succession of convoy runs and bombardments. On 30 September 1940 *Stuart* and the British *Diamond* attacked the Italian submarine *Gondar* north-west of Alexandria, and had the satisfaction of seeing their prey surface and surrender before sinking. Waller sent the classic signal, 'On passage, detected, hunted and sank Italian submarine.' Although these old destroyers had no official role in the front line on account of their great age, the shortage of destroyers resulted in the 10th Flotilla serving as fleet destroyers. Waller had taken the *Stuart* into action against the Italian Fleet at the Battle of Calabria in July 1940, but in March of the following year, she was to take part in that rarest of actions, a torpedo-attack on the enemy fleet. In all their years of service this privilege was only to come the way of the 'V & W' class once again.

In March 1941 the situation in the Mediterranean was critical, for the Luftwaffe had evened the score after Taranto by putting the Mediterranean Fleet's only armoured carrier, the *Illustrious*, out of action. Her replacement, the *Formidable* had arrived, but the Navy had been forced to assume a new commitment, the covering of a British expeditionary force to Greece. The outcome of the Greek campaign was to be disastrous, but even without this knowledge the most sanguine planners realized that the time was ripe for an Italian naval offensive against the exposed British flank. With the Luftwaffe and the Regia Aeronautica in deadly partnership, the threat to Admiral Cunningham's control of the Mediterranean was increasing, and a decisive stroke by Italian heavy units could have severed the link between Greece and Alexandria.

Cunningham was not the man to skulk in Alexandria while the despised Italians planned a raid on his supply-lines, so on the evening of 27 March he took the battle fleet to sea from Alexandria. Aerial reconnaissance indicated that an Italian cruiser-squadron was at sea between Sicily and Crete, and it was Cunningham's intention to intercept it. *Stuart* accompanied the battleships and the carrier, but her flotilla-mate *Vendetta* was screening Vice-Admiral Pridham-Wippell's force of four cruisers. Unfortunately *Vendetta* let down the 'V & W' class reputation for reliability by developing engine-trouble, and was told to return to Alexandria. *Stuart*, however, re-mained to take part in the ensuing action and win renown.

The story of the Battle of Cape Matapan is too well known to be retold in full, but *Stuart*'s part in it can be taken up from the point where Cunningham learnt that his carrier aircraft had damaged the Italian cruiser *Pola*. It was dusk on the evening of 28 March, the sea was calm and visibility was good. Half the destroyers were sent off to search for the Italians, while *Stuart* and her division were kept as a screen for the battleships. Later the battleships stumbled on two Italian cruisers trying to find the crippled *Pola*; *Warspite*, *Valiant* and *Barham* poured 15-inch broadsides into them, and stunned on-lookers in *Stuart* saw the *Fiume* burst into flame instantly. When Italian destroyers tried to attack with torpedoes Cunningham un-leashed his own, and *Stuart* and *Havock* tore in to attack the cruisers. The Australian destroyer fired her torpedoes at the *Zara* and another unidentified ship, then engaged a destroyer. She slid mutely past an Italian cruiser which must have mistaken her for a friend, and went off to fire a few salvoes at the *Zara*, which was burning fiercely.

To Cunningham, reared in destroyers, it seemed as if his victory had been achieved at a cost of heavy destroyer casualties, but as dawn came all the scattered screen reappeared, as the official account put it, 'steaming in two divisions with the slightly self-conscious precision of a peace-time review'.

Although the sequel to Matapan, the consecutive evacuations of Greece and Crete, was an unrelieved series of losses to the Navy, Cun-ningham's victory meant that the Italian Fleet had no stomach for intervention, and was happy to leave the work of destroying British sea power to their air force and the Luftwaffe.

All the Australian destroyers took part in the evacuations, with their British sisters. Only one 'V & W' was lost, the A.A. escort *Wryneck*, which had been detached from the Rosyth Escort Force to strengthen the Mediterranean Fleet. The story of her loss is a harrowing example of the ordeal of ships at the mercy of aircraft.

On Sunday 27 April 1941 the troop transport *Slamat* and *Khedive Ismail* were steaming away from Greece, in the Gulf of Nauplia, accompanied by the A.A. cruiser *Calcutta* and the destroyers *Isis, Hotspur* and *Diamond*. These were the last ships to leave, having left it as long as possible in order to embark as many Australian soldiers as possible at Tolon. At about 0700 the little force was attacked by German dive-bombers, which concentrated on the *Slamat*, larger of the two transports. For ten minutes the aircraft hammered away, until two bombs hit the *Slamat* and stopped her dead. The *Diamond* rescued as many survivors as she could, while the other ships drew away, still under heavy attack from Ju 88 bombers.

As the last Ju 88 dropped its bombs and headed for home the destroyers *Wryneck, Vendetta* and *Waterhen* came up at full speed from the south to take over the task of screening the convoy, and to allow the *Hotspur* and *Isis* to land the soldiers who were crowding their decks. As *Wryneck* had the best anti-aircraft armament of the three destroyers, the captain of the *Calcutta* ordered her to join *Diamond* and pick up more survivors from the *Slamat*, as she was hard-pressed.

When the *Wryneck* found her fellow-destroyer, she had more than 500 survivors on board, but there were still a number of rafts and boats around, and *Wryneck* quickly picked up another 150 men. After torpedoing the *Slamat* both ships headed south again at high speed. At about noon they appear to have been surprised by enemy aircraft which were mistaken for R.A.F. machines. Whether this was a genuine mistake due to peculiar light conditions, or a case of Axis aircraft using R.A.F. roundels will never be known, but the fact remains that survivors claimed that they did not fire because they felt that the planes were Hurricanes.

Even if the guns' crews had opened fire earlier, the result was inevitable. First to go was the *Diamond*, after her packed decks had been raked by machine-gun fire; three bombs blew her apart. Although the *Wryneck* had no chance to bring her 4-inch high-angle guns into action (the only weapons which had any chance of breaking up the attack) she had a moment's grace to open up with her ·5-inch machine-guns before she was destroyed in similar manner. Only one officer, forty-one ratings and eight soldiers survived from the thousand men who had been aboard the three ships.

The Australian destroyers served with distinction during the withdrawal to Crete and the debacle which followed. During 1941 they became regular habitués of the 'Tobruk Run', escorting the nightly supply-runs from Alexandria to Tobruk. The dangers from air-attack were overwhelming, and *Waterhen* was the first of the 'Scrapiron Flotilla' to go; badly battered by German and Italian bombers off Sollum on 29 June 1941, she stayed afloat, but sank in tow the next day. The little 'Chook' had earned a great reputation among the Tobruk garrison for her audacity, and many Australians mourned her loss.

After Pearl Harbour many R.A.N. ships were withdrawn from the Mediterranean, and sent to the Far East, where ships were desperately needed to stem the apparently irresistible tide of Japanese military power. The *Vampire* had been sent back to Australia back in May 1941, as part of the slow process of reinforcement, and the others followed one by one.

When two Japanese carrier task forces penetrated the Indian Ocean in March 1942, the situation facing the Allies was extremely dangerous. Admiral Somerville's scratch force was badly outclassed by the Japanese, and neither Trincomalee nor Colombo offered a secure base. In the words of the official Admiralty historian, Captain Roskill, 'we may be thankful that they [the Japanese] never found him'.[1] If the main Japanese forces had encountered the British Far Eastern Fleet there can be no doubt that they would have annihilated Somerville's three carriers and five battleships.

What happened was bad enough. On the afternoon of 8 April 1942 a Catalina aircraft sighted a large Japanese force (under Admiral Nagumo) about 400 miles east of Ceylon, and heading for the island. That night the order was given to clear all shipping out of Trincomalee harbour, as a heavy carrier strike was expected. The old carrier *Hermes* was given the Australian *Vampire* as escort, and with several

1. *The War at Sea*, Vol. II, p. 27.

naval auxiliaries, was told to head south, hugging the coast. When the attack materialized, the harbour was empty, and the only damage inflicted was on shore installations. The *Hermes* and her small force were about sixty-five miles away at the time, and at about 9 a.m. on 9 April they put about and headed back to Trincomalee. An hour-and-a-half later, having been sighted by a Japanese reconnaissance plane, they were attacked in strength; *Hermes* was the main target, and was rapidly sunk, but the *Vampire*, the corvette *Hollyhock* and two tankers followed her to the bottom. Fortunately a nearby hospital ship, the *Vita*, rescued over 600 survivors. By a strange coincidence, the *Waterhen* had rescued the crew of the *Vita* off Tobruk the previous year, after she had been damaged by Stukas.

There were now only three of the 'Scrapiron Flotilla' left. All three remained in Australian waters, on escort duty. *Voyager* ran aground in Bentano Bay, on the island of Timor, on 23 September 1942; Japanese aircraft soon found her, and inflicted heavy damage, so the ship's company, with no hope of repairing their ship, completed the enemy's work by wrecking the hull. The *Stuart* and *Vendetta* were showing signs of old age, and gradually sank to second-line duties. In 1944 the *Stuart* was partially disarmed and used as a high-speed transport to ferry perishables to the Australian troops fighting in New Guinea, and was still engaged on this humdrum but vital task until early in 1946. The *Vendetta* was spared the humiliation of going to the breaker's yard, for on 2 July 1948 she was scuttled off Sydney Heads, and joined other illustrious Australian warships, including the battlecruiser *Australia*.

# Chapter 8

# 'V & W' WEAPONS

WITH the exception of the 'Wairs', which were armed with the latest pattern of 4-inch twin high-angle guns, the class generally kept its original weapons. Until well into 1940 the standard armament of old 4-inch Mk V or 4·7-inch Mk I remained in position, but after experience in Norway and during the evacuation of the B.E.F. from France, virtually all units but the 'Wairs' surrendered their after set of torpedo-tubes to make room for a 3-inch high-angle gun. A few of the old leaders mounted a 4-inch, since their greater beam allowed the extra weight, and others, such as the *Keppel*, kept all six torpedo-tubes.

As with the 'Wairs' the chief drawback was the lack of a suitable close-range anti-aircraft weapon; the 3-inch or the twin 4-inch could not train fast enough, nor was there a control system which could provide the information, to deal with dive-bombers or fighters which came in close. Only the *Wallace* could take a four-barrelled pom-pom aft, in an ideal position to deal with attacks from astern, which soon became the favourite angle of attack for German pilots. The quadruple ·5-inch machine-gun mounting proved inadequate, whereas the old single 2-pounder pom-poms sited abaft the funnels proved to be effective, and were doubled, in positions winged out on either beam. The new 20-mm. Oerlikon gun showed great promise, but as production was painfully slow it was clear that elderly destroyers must wait for a long time before any could be spared.[1] The ·5-inch machine-guns were still in some ships in mid-1942, but after that time they

1. An Admiralty list of armaments shows *Valentine* armed with 4 × 20-mm. guns in 1940. This vessel completed her 'Wair' conversion in March 1940 and was sunk two months later, but as her sisters a year later were only allowed *two* Oerlikons, one can only assume that a provision of four weapons for 'V & W' destroyers was a pious intention.

were all replaced by two single 20-mm. guns. In the early days of the war a number of twin Lewis guns were mounted in various ships, but they did not last for very long.

In all the unconverted destroyers the next step was to remove 'X' gun from the quarterdeck to make space for large depth-charge racks, as well as four depth-charge throwers with handling equipment. The former magazine and shellroom for 'X' gun was converted to depth-charge stowage; in those ships which had additional depth-charge throwers mounted forward of the after superstructure, stowage was also provided on deck. When one reads of destroyers on escort duty in the Battle of the Atlantic one should always remember the depth-charge crews, huddled aft on a quarterdeck swept by wind and sea, wrestling with the unwieldy 300 lb. charges as they were loaded on to the throwers; frequently the speed with which the throwers were reloaded proved decisive in following up a successful Asdic contact, and the depth-charge crews had one of the hardest jobs of all.

In March 1942 a new type of depth-charge, known as the Mark 10, was introduced. It was a 1-ton charge, intended to deal with deep-diving U-boats, and also designed to overcome the delay between loss of Asdic contact and the firing of depth-charges. The earlier patterns of Asdic had a relatively narrow beam which lost contact if the pursuing destroyer closed with and over-ran the target; later this problem was solved by introducing a second set which could hold the target in the vertical plane more successfully, but this refinement was only available in later ships. With the normal pattern of Asdic the hunting ship lost contact and completed her run-in and attack by guesswork on the part of her captain; the delay as the depth-charges sank to their preset firing depth thus contributed to the possibility of error.

The idea of a super-charge was examined in 1938, largely with a view to increasing the lethal range of the Mk 7 depth-charge; the original solution was to link three Mk 7 charges, but work on the project was abandoned until January 1941, when the new Staff requirement was put forward. This time a 1-ton charge was designed for firing from existing torpedo-tubes, and after a number of teething troubles it was fitted in the destroyers *Ambuscade, Boadicea, Buxton, Chesterfield* and *Newmarket*. At first C.O.s of escorts were understandably nervous of using such a large charge, despite the fact that trials had shown that it was safe at a speed of eleven knots or more. After modification to improve its rate of sinking it became the Mk 10*, and was used against targets at 600 feet or more. It was subsequently proved to be usable at 900 feet or more, even if the ship was stationary.

Most of the modernized 'V & W' escorts retained one set of triple tubes to fire two Mk 10 and one Mk 10* depth-charges.[1] The total weight of each charge was 3,000 lb. and contained 2,000 lb. of explosive. The safe laying speed was fixed at eighteen knots minimum in order to reduce the risk of damage to the ship. In 1944 an improved pattern, the Mk 10**, was given even greater speed of sinking, and the maximum depth-setting was increased to 1,500 feet, to take account of the phenomenal depths reached by desperate U-boat commanders. One or two intrepid German submariners had taken their boats far beyond their designed diving-depth, and Allied escort commanders found that the normal depth-charge setting had not allowed for this.

Apart from U-boats, the major scourge of convoys in the Channel and on the East Coast routes was the German M.T.B. or *Schnellboot*, better known as the E-boat. It proved a very tough antagonist, for it was fast and had a low silhouette, making it a difficult target. In addition the E-boats' diesel engines made them far less prone to catch fire than their British counterparts. The standard destroyer guns, whether 4-inch or 4·7-inch, were too slow in training and rate of fire to enable them to engage targets which slid out of the darkness to dart across their bows and disappear again. The Oerlikon gun was useful, but as it fired only a 20mm. shell it could do little vital damage.

The first remedy against E-boats was to fit a single 2-pounder pom-pom on the forecastle, right in the eyes of the ship to give a clear field of fire at maximum depression port and starboard. This mounting was also sometimes used for firing starshell. By 1944 a formidable weapon had appeared, a power-operated 6-pounder twin-barrelled mounting capable of as much as eighty rounds per minute. It had originally been designed for the Army as a coast-defence weapon,

1. The Mk 10* charge was always fired from the right-hand torpedo-tube.

despite its lack of range. It proved very effective at Malta in July 1941, when it helped to break up an attack by Italian M.T.B.s, and in 1943 a number were supplied to the Navy. After modification to improve the mounting for naval service it was adopted as the 6-pdr. Twin Mk 1, and mounted in 'A' position in the *Walpole, Windsor, Whitshed, Wivern, Mackay* and *Montrose*.

## PARTICULARS OF 6-PDR. TWIN MK 1

| | |
|---|---|
| *Rate of Fire* | 80 rounds per min. maximum |
| | 72 rounds per min. normal |
| *lbs. output* | 432 per minute |
| *Maximum Range* | 5,150 yards |
| *No. of crew* | 8 ratings plus control number |
| *Weight* | 10 cwt. |

Compared with these figures, the 4·7-inch B.L. Mk 1 mounted in the Modified 'Ws' and leaders could only fire six rounds per minute, totalling 300 lb. of shells; the range was 16,000 yards, but against E-boats volume of fire at short range was far more important. In addition, the 6-pounder twin was capable of blind fire with the aid of Type 271 or 272 radar.

When the Long Range Escort conversion was introduced, the 'V & W' escorts taken in hand were given a new anti-submarine weapon, the 'Hedgehog'. This was a spigot mortar which fired twenty-four bombs ahead of the ship; each bomb had a warhead with 32 pounds of Torpex, a new powerful explosive, fused to burst only on contact. The 'Hedgehog' was the first weapon introduced to counter-act the problem mentioned earlier, that of loss of Asdic contact as the ship ran over the target. By firing a salvo of twenty-four bombs ahead, the escort could remain in contact longer, and increase the chances of a 'kill'. 'Hedgehog' tactics took some time to perfect, and they never replaced the conventional method of dropping patterns of depth-charges, but they were an important step forward. The name was derived from the rows of bombs resting at an angle on their spigots, like the spines of a hedgehog. It is interesting to note that in 1941 *Whitehall* was given an experimental armament of four depth-

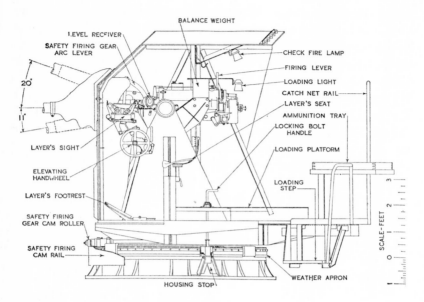

BALANCE WEIGHT

LEVEL RECEIVER

SAFETY FIRING GEAR
ARC LEVER

CHECK FIRE LAMP

FIRING LEVER

LOADING LIGHT

CATCH NET RAIL

LAYER'S SEAT

AMMUNITION TRAY

LOCKING BOLT
HANDLE

20°

11°

LAYER'S SIGHT

LOADING PLATFORM

ELEVATING
HANDWHEEL

LAYER'S FOOTREST

LOADING
STEP

SAFETY FIRING
GEAR CAM ROLLER

SAFETY FIRING
CAM RAIL

SCALE-FEET

3

2

1

0

HOUSING STOP

WEATHER APRON

## LEFT SIDE ELEVATION

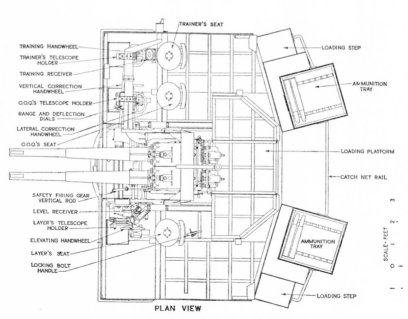

TRAINER'S SEAT

TRAINING HANDWHEEL

TRAINER'S TELESCOPE
HOLDER

TRAINING RECEIVER

VERTICAL CORRECTION
HANDWHEEL

O.O.Q'S TELESCOPE HOLDER

RANGE AND DEFLECTION
DIALS

LATERAL CORRECTION
HANDWHEEL

O.O.Q'S SEAT

SAFETY FIRING GEAR
VERTICAL ROD

LEVEL RECEIVER

LAYER'S TELESCOPE
HOLDER

ELEVATING HANDWHEEL

LAYER'S SEAT

LOCKING BOLT
HANDLE

LOADING STEP

AMMUNITION
TRAY

LOADING PLATFORM

CATCH NET RAIL

AMMUNITION
TRAY

LOADING STEP

SCALE-FEET

3

2

1

0

1

## PLAN VIEW

89

charge throwers abreast in 'A' position, to provide ahead-throwing.

A number of escorts were also altered to enable them to lay much larger patterns of depth-charges. With four throwers and a single rack of depth-charges, the standard pattern was five charges, but in some vessels additional depth-charge racks and throwers increased the pattern to fourteen charges. As greater numbers of 20-mm. Oerlikon guns became available the 12-pounder anti-aircraft gun was removed, and the space was converted to enlarged depth-charge stowage. In a long Atlantic convoy battle destroyers used depth-charges at a prodigious rate, and it was often necessary to replenish stocks in mid-Atlantic.

In their final guise the 'V & W' escorts would have a typical armament as follows :

*'A' position*—'Hedgehog.'
*'B' position*—4-inch or 4.7-inch gun (original weapon).
*Bridge wings*—single 20-mm. guns port and starboard.
*Abaft funnels*—two single 2-pounders or 20-mm. A.A., port and starboard, one set triple torpedo-tubes, additional depth-charge stowage, and possibly additional throwers.
*'X' position*—4-inch or 4.7-inch as 'B'.
*'Y' position*—two depth-charge racks discharging over quarterdeck, and two depth-charge throwers on each side, with associated stowage and davits for reloading; additional 20-mm. A.A. gun in some ships.

In addition there would be surface warning radar on the bridge, air warning radar at the masthead, and a high-frequency direction-finding aerial on a specially rigged mainmast.

The distribution of armament shown above would apply to a Long Range or Short Range Escort; the 'Wairs' were simpler in layout, having only their twin 4-inch A.A. guns forward and aft, and by 1942, single 20-mm. guns in the bridge wings and amidships (either abreast or staggered), and a more modest outfit of depth-charges on the quarterdeck. The *Wallace* was the only 'Wair' to differ, since she had a four-barrelled pom-pom aft, and had to accommodate her depth-charge equipment further forward. In addition, owing to her greater size, she had two additional 2-pounder single pom-poms mounted on the upper deck amidships.

The remaining leaders were unconverted, and continued to serve as Short Range Escorts (a report that *Keppel* became a Long Range Escort has not been confirmed, although it was approved). Their lay-out was non-standard, and in one or two cases a 4-inch A.A. gun was mounted in place of the 12-pounder, sometimes in its original (prewar) position, but sometimes in 'X' position. One or two also re-tained their full set of six torpedo-tubes for use against surface forces.

Although neither can be classed as weapons, both radar and High-frequency Direction-finding (Huff-Duff') played such a vital part that they cannot be omitted from any assessment of anti-submarine weapons. Both played a vital role, complementing Asdic and making anti-submarine tactics more effective. Radar, or as it was always known in British parlance until late in the war, R.D.F. or Radio Direction-finding, was introduced in its surface-warning form. The most usual set was the 271 type, with its distinctive 'lantern' housing on the bridge in place of the old rangefinder. Later Type 291, an air-warning set, was added, and was identifiable by the 'X' aerial at the masthead. In some of the leaders and Modified 'W' type the surface-warning radar lantern was mounted on a small lattice-tower aft. In addition to providing surface search capabilities, Type 271 was eventually capable of providing information for laying the twin 6-pounder mentioned earlier, but in general the fire-control of the 'V & W' class remained as crude as it had been before 1939, and if anything was worse in ships which sacrificed their range-finders and pedestal directors to make way for radar sets.

As the war progressed various ships were fitted with new marks of R.D.F., but these were merely refinements of the basic 271 and 291 sets. Some ships also received lesser refinements such as the American-designed T.B.S., or 'Talk Between Ships', a V.H.F. voice transmission wireless set which enabled the escort commander to 'talk' to his escorts. The tedious process of calling-up escorts by lamp was elimin-ated by T.B.S., giving an obvious advantage in co-ordination of escort tactics.

'Huff-Duff' proved to be the vital element in defeating the U-boats' 'wolf-pack' system. If a single U-boat was shadowing a convoy, and sending out homing signals to other U-boats, any means of finding and sinking the shadower, or merely forcing him to submerge, would frustrate the wolf-pack; there would be a delay until another shadower located the convoy and directed the rest of the pack to its prey. If two escorts fitted with 'Huff-Duff' were present with the convoy they could obtain cross-bearings on the shadower and attack him. Skilled operators learned to distinguish between the V.H.F. ground-wave and sky-wave transmissions from U-boats, and could estimate the position of the U-boat. In many cases escort commanders were given warning of an imminent attack merely by learning that the U-boats had located their convoy; this allowed the convoy to make a drastic alteration of course, while the escorts carried out an attack to sink or scare off the shadower.

# Chapter 9

# EPILOGUE

By 1945 the sixty-eight destroyers of the various groups had suffered seventeen war losses, exactly 25 per cent of their strength. Nine were sunk by air attack, five by torpedo, two by mine, and only one, the *Broke*, by gunfire. She had been detailed with the *Malcolm* to land assault troops at Algiers in 1942; after heavy losses from shore batteries the *Malcolm* withdrew, but the *Broke* went on to penetrate the boom and land her troops. She was too heavily damaged to survive, however, and she sank in tow next day.

Shortage of space precludes a list of all the damage suffered by the 'V & W' destroyers during World War II, for it is a long one; ships were hit in dock, and at sea, or had minor collisions with other destroyers. Practically every ship of the class suffered damage of some sort during the war, and yet they continued to serve with as much reliability as destroyers built ten years later. Not until 1944 were any of the class found to be beyond economical repair; the *Worcester*, *Walpole* and *Wrestler* were all damaged between December 1943 and January 1945, and written off as constructional total losses, but when the 'Wair' *Wolfhound* was broken in two by a stick of bombs in September 1941, she was given a refit at Chatham lasting nearly eighteen months.

The *Wivern*, known as the 'Tiddley Wiv', went to the rescue of the torpedoed Canadian corvette *Weyburn*. Unfortunately the corvette's depth-charges had been set for 25 feet, and these went off as she sank alongside the *Wivern*; all engines and boilers were lifted off their mountings, and the ship was completely out of action. In her case the refit at Devonport Dockyard also took seventeen months, and she was fitted for East Coast convoy duties, with a twin 6-pounder in 'A' position. Her only difficulty after her heavy damage was with her steering engine, which tended to shake itself loose. This was normally cured by a stoker who knocked wedges in between the engine and the bulkhead from time to time. Her only nasty moment came in a Force 12 gale off Newcastle in 1945, when a weld on the ship's bottom (part of the original repairs) cracked under the strain, and allowed the forward magazines to flood. In spite of a tremendous weight of water up forward she weathered the storm and returned to port safely next morning.

In July 1945 the 'Wairs' began to be laid up in reserve at Grangemouth. Their 4-inch high-angle guns were removed and installed in the new 'Bay' class frigates then commissioning, but the disarmed hulks lay around for some time, and many did not reach the breakers finally until 1948. The *Winchester* had been laid up as an accommodation ship at Rosyth from February 1945, and the Short Range Escort *Witch* had been used for minesweeping trials since December 1944. Other ships, such as the leader *Montrose*, were laid up after minor damage; in her case she had been damaged in collision with an American ship off Normandy in June 1944, but the pressure on dockyard resources was so great that she and the *Wrestler*, which had been mined on the same day, were immediately paid off.

So far as can be traced, the last 'V & W' in commission was the *Witch*, as she carried out minesweeping trials at Rosyth until the end of June 1946. When she paid off she brought to an end a tradition of twenty-nine years of service which the *Valkyrie* began in June 1917. With the 'V & W' class went most of the pre-war destroyers as well. The fleet destroyer reached its zenith of development in World War II, and the 'V & Ws' were not outlasted for many more years by their modern sisters. Today the fleet destroyer has given way to the frigate, and the Royal Navy's last destroyers are for disposal, yet there are many people alive today who knew the 'V & W' class in 1917. The time scale is not immense, but these destroyers represent somehow a different Navy, different ships, different attitudes, and even a different way of building ships.

# PART TWO
## APPENDICES

One of the few views of *Woolston* as a 'Wair', taken in April 1940. Note that she differs from *Viceroy* in retaining her Thornycroft-style after funnel. She also differs in having single 2-pdr. pom-poms staggered to port and starboard fore-and-aft of the searchlight.

*Wolsey*, unlike *Viceroy* and *Woolston*, was typical of the 'Wair' type in having quadruple machine guns amidships (in some 'Wairs' the mountings were placed on the centre line fore-and-aft of the searchlight).

Two views of *Wolfhound*, showing details of her 'Wair' refit.

*Vanessa* at Blackwall on completion of her refit as a Long Range Escort in April 1942. Note the 'Hedgehog' spigot mortar covered by canvas, underneath the blast shield to 'B' gun.

The former 'Modified W' *Vansittart* in May 1943 after conversion to Long Range Escort.

Three views of *Verity*:

(1) (*Above*) Evoking memories of Dunkirk as she embarks soldiers during the evacuation from Greece in 1941.

(2) (*Centre*) As a Short Range Escort, with minor alterations to her anti-aircraft armament, and 'Y' gun replaced by depth charges, but the old range finder still in place on the bridge.

(3) (*Below*) As a Long Range Escort in November 1943, with all tubes removed; five 20-mm Oerlikons, including one on the quarterdeck and two at split levels abaft No. 2 funnel.

None of the seven 'Modified Ws' with the thick funnel foremost were altered to Long Range Escorts, owing to the awkward arrangement of boilers. *Veteran* and her sisters remained short on endurance, but as this photograph shows, they were powerfully armed. Note, from l. to r.: 'Hedgehog' mortar, 4·7-in. gun, surface warning radar, 2-pounder pom-poms port and starboard, triple torpedo tubes for firing 1-ton depth charges, 12-pdr. high-angle gun, 4·7-in. gun, and twin Lewis machine guns port and starboard on the quarterdeck.

The Long Range Escort *Wanderer* alongside a fleet oiler during a North Atlantic convoy operation. She is replenishing her depth charges after heavy expenditure in action.

The old leader *Wallace* was the only one of either the *Scott* or *Shakespeare* classes turned into a 'Wair'. These three views show how her funnels distinguished her from other 'Wairs', as well as the quadruple pom-pom right aft and the Type 272 radar lantern on its tower amidships. The third view shows her in February 1944, by which time her quadruple ·5-inch machine guns had been replaced by a pair of single 2-pdr. pom-poms.

A fine view of the *Watchman* as a Long Range Escort, showing her 'bow-chaser' 2-pdr. pom-pom right forward.

*Whitehall* in 1941 was experimentally armed with four large calibre mortars in place of 'A' gun. This appears to have been part of the development of the 'Hedgehog' and 'Squid' weapons, but it was not successful, and was removed when the ship became a Long Range Escort in 1942.

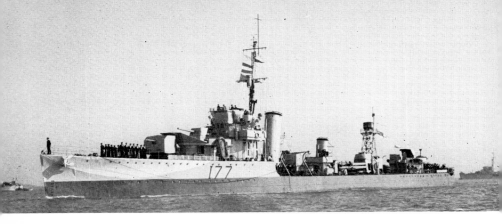

*Whitshed* mounted the twin 6-pdr. gun already seen in the photograph of *Montrose*. As this view shows it was a bulky mounting for the size of gun.

Two sisters, *Whitshed* (left) and *Worcester* (right) at Harwich, the base from which they attacked the German battle-cruisers *Scharnhorst* and *Gneisenau* in 1941. Note that both ships still retain 'Y' gun on the quarterdeck; the added depth charge throwers are mounted between the searchlight position and the after deckhouse.

# APPENDICES

## ABBREVIATIONS

BU    = Broken Up/Scrapped
SHP    = Shaft Horsepower
Q.F.    = Quickfirer (i.e. a gun using 'fixed' ammunition)
C.P.    = Centre Pivot (applied to old gun-mountings)
DY    = Dockyard
oa    = overall (total length of ship)
pp    = b.p., between perpendiculars (length of ship between forefoot and rudderpost)
p.s.i.    = per square inch (boiler-pressure)
pdr.    = pounder (type of gun designated by weight of shell)
T.T.    = Torpedo-tubes

*Group I*—'V' Class Leaders

| name | builder | laid down | launched | completed |
|---|---|---|---|---|
| *Valentine* | Cammell Laird | 7 Aug '16 | 24 Mar '17 | 27 June '17 |
| *Valhalla* | do. | 8 Aug '16 | 22 May '17 | 31 July '17 |
| *Valkyrie* (ex-*Montrose*) | Wm. Denny | 25 May '16 | 13 Mar '17 | 16 June '17 |
| *Valorous* (ex-*Malcolm*) | do. | 25 May '16 | 8 May '17 | 21 Aug '17 |
| *Vampire* (ex-*Wallace*) | J. S. White | 10 Oct '16 | 21 May '17 | 22 Sept '17 |

*Displacement*: 1,457 tons (legend), 1,473 tons (full load) 1,188 tons (standard).
*Dimensions*: 300' (pp) 312' (oa) × 29' 6" × 10' 8" (min)/11' 7½" max.
*Machinery*: Three Yarrow (except *Vampire* White-Forster) boilers, 250 lb/in²; two shafts; Brown-Curtis (except *Valorous* and *Valkyrie* Parsons) SR geared turbines; S.H.P. 27,000 = 34 knots.
*Bunkers* and *Radius*: O.F. 185 tons (load draught), 367 tons (max); 3,500 miles @ 15 knots.
*Armament*: Four 4-inch Q.F. on CP.II mountings (30 deg elevation),

one 3-inch H.A. 20 cwt Mk III guns (see notes for alterations); four (except *Vampire* six) 21-inch T.T. (2 × 2/3 – four/six torpedoes).
*Complement*: 115 (later increased to 134).

*Notes*: Original armament as designed was single 4-inch guns on P.X. mountings with 25 deg elevation; 120 rounds carried for each 4-inch, 100 for 3-inch. *Circa* 1920 *Valentine* and *Valorous* armed with triple torpedo-tubes in place of twins; re-armed 1938–39 with four 4-inch A.A. (2 × 2), eight ·5-inch MGs (2 × 4) and HA.DCTs. *Valkyrie* and *Valhalla* had their twin T.T.s replaced by triples in 1925, and all but *Valhalla* had their 3-inch H.A. gun replaced by a 2-pounder A.A.

The two Denny boats were ordered in April 1916, and the others in July 1916. After 1920 all were re-rated as ordinary destroyers, having been divisional, or 'half', leaders since 1919. The main difference between the 'V' leaders of this group and the later destroyers of the class was in the internal arrangement of accommodation to allow for the presence of Captain (D) and his staff on board. When the ships were disrated this accommodation was retained; e.g. the *Vampire* often served as a leader when the R.A.N. leader *Stuart* was not in commission.

*Appearance*: As built all differed from the standard 'V & W' boats in having the standard compass forward of the searchlight platform. This distinguishing feature disappeared from *Valentine* and *Valorous* when they became 'Wairs' in 1938–40 (see later).

*Group II*—Thornycroft Leaders

| name | builder | laid down | launched | completed |
|---|---|---|---|---|
| *Rooke* | Thornycroft | Nov '18 | 16 Sept '20 | 20 Jan '25* |
| *Keppel* | do. | Oct '18 | 23 Apr '20 | 15 Apr '25† |
| *Saunders* | do. | Cancelled 12 April 1919 | | |
| *Shakespeare* | do. | Oct '16 | 7 July '17 | 10 Oct '17 |
| *Spenser* | do. | Oct '16 | 22 Sept '17 | Dec '17 |
| *Spragge* | do. | Cancelled 12 April 1919 | | |
| *Wallace* | do. | Aug '17 | 26 Oct '18 | Feb '19 |
| *Barrington | Cammell Laird | Cancelled 26 November 1918 | | |
| † *Hughes* | do. | Cancelled 26 November 1918 | | |

* Completed by Pembroke Dockyard (renamed *Broke* 13 Apr 1921).
† Completed by Portsmouth Dockyard.

*Displacement*: 1,554 tons (standard).

*Dimensions*: 318′ (pp) 329′ (oa) × 31′ 6″ × 12′ 4″ (mean).

*Machinery*: Four Yarrow boilers, 250 lb/in²; two shafts; Brown-Curtis all-geared turbines; S.H.P. 40,000 = 36 knots.

*Bunkers* and *Radius*: O.F. 250 tons (normal), 500 tons (max); 5,000 miles @ 15 knots.

*Armament*: Five 4·7-inch B.L. Mk I on CP VI mountings (30 deg elevation), one 3-inch H.A. Mk III, two 2-pounder pom-poms, guns; six 21-inch (2 × 3) T.T.

*Complement*: 183.

*Notes*: Original armament proposed was five 5-inch or six 4-inch, but finally a naval version of the Army 4·7-inch field gun (45 lb shell, separate charge) was adopted; the planned A.A. armament of two 2-pounders was replaced by a 3-inch H.A. gun before completion, but the pom-poms were re-sited on the upper deck near the after superstructure. Outfit of ammunition for 4·7-inch as in 'V' leaders, but 3-inch outfit increased to 190 rounds per gun.

In August 1917 a 9-ft rangefinder, torpedo control gear, and fore-bridge firing was approved for the class, marking a big improvement in fire-control for ships of this size.

Two ships marked ‡, *Barrington* and *Hughes*, were ordered to be built to the Thornycroft design but in another yard, the only time this was done. The contracts were cancelled as it was felt that Cammell Laird might not have been able to achieve the spectacular savings in weight which were a feature of all Thornycroft designs, when working with unfamiliar types; the work had only been given to Cammell Laird on account of the Woolston yard being fully extended in the spring of 1918. *Shakespeare* and *Spenser* ordered April 1916, *Wallace* in April 1917, and the others in April 1918.

*Service 1939–45*: Only three survived to 1939 (see later notes).

*Appearance*: Their high freeboard and typical flat-sided Thornycroft funnels gave them an impressive silhouette, especially as the funnels appeared to be set farther aft than usual. This feature was retained when the *Wallace* become a 'Wair', but the *Broke* lost her Thornycroft look at the beginning of the War (see later notes).

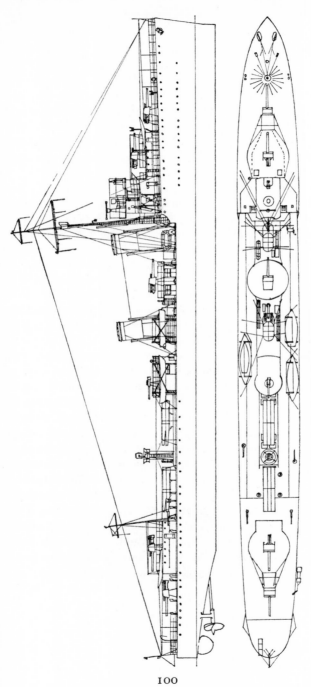

*Broke* (Shakespeare Class) as built

*Group III*—Admiralty Leaders

| name | builder | laid down | launched | completed |
|------|---------|-----------|----------|-----------|
| *Bruce* | Cammell Laird | 12 May '17 | 26 Feb '18 | 29 May '18 |
| *Campbell* | do. | 10 Nov '17 | 21 Sept '18 | 21 Dec '18 |
| *Douglas* | do | 30 June '17 | 8 June '18 | 30 Aug '18 |
| *Mackay* (ex-*Claverhouse*) | do. | 5 Mar '18 | 21 Dec '18 | June '19 |
| *Malcolm* | do. | 27 Mar '18 | 29 May '19 | 14 Dec '19 |
| *Montrose* | do. | 4 Oct '17 | 10 June '18 | 14 Sep '18 |
| *Scott* | do. | 19 Feb '17 | 18 Oct '17 | 16 Jan '18 |
| *Stuart* | do. | 18 Oct '17 | 22 Aug '18 | 21 Dec '18 |

*Displacement*: 1,530 tons (standard).

*Dimensions*: 320'(pp), 332' 6"(oa) × 31' 9" × 12' (max).

*Machinery*: Four Yarrow boilers, 250 lb/in²; two shafts; Parsons all-geared turbines (except *Montrose* and *Stuart*, Brown-Curtis); S.H.P. 40,000 = 36½ knots.

*Bunkers* and *Radius*: 504 tons (max), 401 tons (normal); 5,000 miles @ 15 knots.

*Armament*: Five 4·7-inch, etc., as Group II.

*Complement*: 183.

*Notes*: The original armament was revised as for Group II. Eight vessels survived to outbreak of World War II, but *Bruce* had been disarmed by 1939 for service as a Fleet Target, and being beyond economical repair was expended as a target in November 1939. The others all served as Short Range Escorts, with the exception of *Stuart*, which had been transferred to the Royal Australian Navy in 1933, and served until 1944 as a fleet destroyer (see later notes). *Scott* ordered April 1916, *Bruce* and *Douglas* in December 1916, and the others in April 1917.

*Appearance*: Like the Thornycroft leaders, this group differed from the standard 'V & W' fleet destroyers by having a fifth gun on a 'band-stand' platform between the funnels. However, they had round funnels instead of the Thornycroft type, which made them look similar to the later 'A' and 'B' class destroyers.

*Group IV*—Admiralty 'V' Class Fleet Destroyers

| name | builder | laid down | launched | completed |
|------|---------|-----------|----------|-----------|
| *Vancouver** | Beardmore | 15 Mar '17 | 28 Dec '17 | 9 Mar '18 |
| *Vanessa* | do. | 16 May '17 | 16 Mar '18 | 27 Apr '18 |
| *Vanity* | do. | 28 July '17 | 3 May '18 | 21 June '18 |
| *Vanoc* | John Brown | 20 Sept '16 | 14 June '17 | 15 Aug '17 |
| *Vanquisher* | do. | 27 Sept '16 | 18 Aug '17 | 2 Oct '17 |
| *Vectis* | J. S. White | 7 Dec '16 | 4 Sept. '17 | 5 Dec. '17 |
| *Vortigern* | do. | 17 Jan '17 | 15 Oct '17 | 25 Jan '18 |
| *Vega* | Doxford | 11 Dec '16 | 1 Sept '17 | Dec '17 |
| *Velox* | do. | Jan '17 | 17 Nov '17 | 1 Apr '18 |
| *Vehement* | Wm. Denny | 25 Sept '16 | 6 July '17 | 16 Oct '17 |
| *Venturous* | do. | 9 Oct '16 | 21 Sept '17 | 29 Nov '17 |
| *Vendetta* | Fairfield | Nov '16 | 3 Sept '17 | 17 Oct '17 |
| *Venetia* | do. | 2 Feb '17 | 29 Oct '17 | 19 Dec '17 |
| *Verdun* | Hawthorn Leslie | 13 Jan '17 | 21 Aug '17 | 3 Nov '17 |
| *Versatile* | do. | 31 Jan '17 | 31 Oct '17 | 11 Feb '18 |
| *Verulam* | do. | 8 Feb '17 | 3 Oct '17 | 12 Dec '17 |
| *Vesper* | Alex. Stephen | 27 Dec '16 | 15 Dec '17 | 20 Feb '18 |
| *Vidette* | do. | 1 Feb '17 | 28 Feb '18 | 27 Apr '18 |
| *Vimiera* | Swan, Hunter | Oct '16 | 22 June '17 | 19 Sept '17 |
| *Violent* | do. | Nov '16 | 1 Sept '17 | Nov '17 |
| *Vittoria* | do. | Feb '17 | 29 Oct '17 | May '18 |
| *Vivacious* | Yarrow | July '16 | 3 Nov '17 | Dec '17 |
| *Vivien* | do. | July '16 | 16 Feb '18 | 28 May '18 |

\* Renamed *Vimy* 1 April 1928 to release name for 'S' class destroyer transferred to Canada.

*Displacement*: 1,090 tons (standard).
*Dimensions*: 300'(pp), 312'(oa) × 29' 6″ × 10' 9″ (load)/11' 7½″ (deep).
*Machinery*: Three Yarrow boilers (except *Vectis* and *Vortigern*, White-Forster); two shafts; Brown-Curtis SR geared turbines (except Doxford and Swan Hunter boats, Parsons); S.H.P. 27,000 = 34 knots.
*Bunkers* and *Radius*: 185 tons (load), 368 tons (max); 1,000 miles @ full speed, 3,500 miles @ 15 knots.
*Armament*: Four 4-inch Q.F. Mk V (30 deg elevation), one 3-inch

H.A. [original] replaced subsequently by one 2-pounder pom-pom in most [see notes]; four, five or six 21-inch T.T. (2 × 2/3 or 1 × 2, 1 × 3).

*Complement*: 134.

*Notes*: Differed from Group I only in arrangements internally (no accommodation for Captain (D) and staff) and in minor external points, such as the absence of the compass platform before the searchlight position. All ordered June 1916 except White boats, in August.

As with Group I, T.T. were changed from twin-mountings to triples from 1920 onwards, as time permitted, but the five minelayers *Vanoc, Velox, Versatile, Vimy* (ex-*Vancouver*) and *Vortigern* retained their after-bank of twin tubes, and remained 5-tube boats until 1939. *Vivien* was used for trials and experimental work, and was fitted with a large gyro stabiliser at one stage; *circa* 1923 she was fitted with a single 24½-inch T.T. in place of the after triple mounting for a while.

*Appearance*: The two White boats had distinctive level tops to their forefunnels, the Hawthorn Leslie boats had prominent funnel-caps, and searchlight-platforms differed slightly from builder to builder. The following boats were fitted for minelaying 1917-18, and retained their mine-chutes on the quarterdeck: *Vimy* (ex-*Vancouver*), *Vanoc, Vanquisher, Vehement, Velox, Venetia, Venturous, Versatile, Verulam, Vesper, Vittoria* and *Vivacious*.

*Group V*—Thornycroft 'V' Class

| name | builder | laid down | launched | completed |
|------|---------|-----------|----------|-----------|
| *Viceroy* | Thornycroft | Dec '16 | 17 Nov '17 | Jan '18 |
| *Viscount* | do. | 20 Dec '16 | 29 Dec '17 | 4 Mar '18 |

*Displacement*: 1,120 tons (standard).

*Dimensions*: 300'(pp), 312'(oa) × 30' 8½" × 10' 9" (mean).

*Machinery*: Three Thornycroft boilers; two shafts; Brown-Curtis SR geared turbines; S.H.P. 30,000 = 37 knots.

*Bunkers* and *Radius*: O.F. 322 tons (load), 374 tons (max); as Groups I and IV.

*Armament*: As Groups I and IV.

*Complement*: 134.

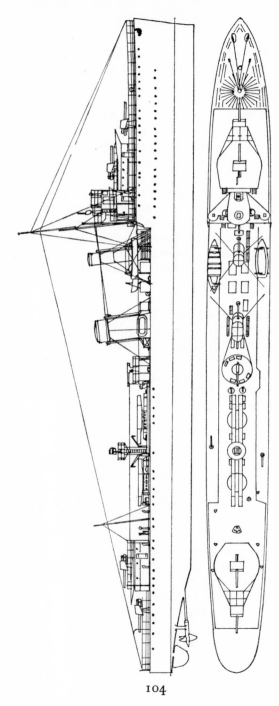

*Viscount* (Thornycroft 'V' Class) as built

APPENDICES

*Notes*: With these two boats the builders were allowed a certain
latitude, in view of their long experience in designing and building
destroyers. The principal difference lay in more powerful machinery,
based on the *Taurus*, Thornycroft's 'R' class; the hull-form was
altered to give higher freeboard and greater beam. Both boats had a
distinctive appearance, with tall flat-sided after-funnels, but armament remained the same as the other 'V & W' boats, and was altered
in the same manner post-1920. Ordered August 1916.
Both boats served in World War II, one as a 'Wair' and the other as
a Long Range Escort.

*Group VI*—Admiralty 'W' Class or Repeat 'V' Class

| name | builder | laid down | launched | completed |
|------|---------|-----------|----------|-----------|
| *Voyager* | Alex. Stephen | 17 May '17 | 8 May '18 | 24 June '18 |
| *Wakeful* | Beardmore | 17 Jan '17 | 6 Oct '17 | Nov '17 |
| *Watchman* | do. | 17 Jan '17 | 2 Nov '17 | 26 Jan '18 |
| *Walker* | Wm. Denny | 26 Mar '17 | 29 Nov '17 | 12 Feb '18 |
| *Westcott* | do. | 30 Mar '17 | 14 Feb '18 | 12 Apr '18 |
| *Walpole* | Doxford | May '17 | 12 Feb '18 | 7 Aug '18 |
| *Whitley* (ex-*Whitby*)* | do. | June '17 | 13 Apr '18 | 14 Oct '18 |
| *Walrus* | Fairfield | Feb '17 | 27 Dec '17 | 8 Mar '18 |
| *Wolfhound* | do. | Apr '17 | 14 Mar '18 | 27 Apr '18 |
| *Warwick* | Hawthorn Leslie | 10 Mar '17 | 28 Dec '17 | 18 Mar '18 |
| *Wessex* | do. | 23 May '17 | 12 Mar '18 | 11 May '18 |
| *Waterhen* | Palmers | July '17 | 26 Mar '18 | 17 Apr '18 |
| *Wryneck* | do. | July '17 | 13 May '18 | 11 Nov '18 |
| *Westminster* | Scotts | Apr '17 | 25 Feb '18 | 18 Apr '18 |
| *Windsor* | do. | Apr '17 | 21 June '18 | 28 Aug '18 |
| *Whirlwind* | Swan Hunter | May '17 | 15 Dec '17 | 15 Mar '18 |
| *Wrestler* | do. | July '17 | 25 Feb '18 | 15 May '18 |
| *Winchelsea* | J. S. White | 24 May '17 | 15 Dec '17 | 15 Mar '18 |
| *Winchester* | do. | 12 June '17 | 1 Feb '18 | 29 Apr '18 |

* Name allocated was *Whitby*, but typing error caused her to be
launched as *Whitley*, and the error was not reversed.

*Displacement*: 1,100 tons (standard).

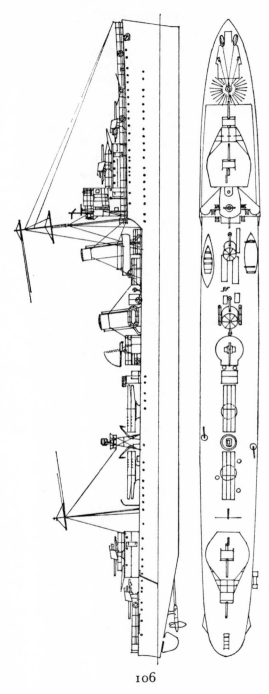

*Wolfhound* ('W' Class) as built

*Dimensions*: As Groups I and IV.

*Machinery*: As Groups I and IV, but Parsons turbines in Palmers' and Swan Hunter's boats, and Brown-Curtis turbines in Doxford boats.

*Bunkers* and *Radius*: As Groups I and IV.

*Armament*: Guns as Groups I and IV: six 21-inch T.T. (2 × 3).

*Complement*: As Group IV.

*Notes*: This group differed from the Admiralty 'V' type (Group IV) in having triple torpedo-tubes, but was otherwise identical.

*Appearance*: As built the only differences were the triple T.T. and a taller mainmast. The two White boats *Winchester* and *Winchelsea* had flat tops to their forefunnels, as *Vectis* and *Vortigern* (q.v., but photographis indicate that they carried funnel extensions at some stage, which altered their silhouette slightly. There were many peacetime alterations of a minor nature, e.g. *Wolfhound* was disarmed for a time, and *Wakeful* had a rangefinder in place of 'A' gun, but these were only temporary.

Those fitted for minelaying in 1918 included: *Walker*, *Walrus*, *Warwick*, *Watchman* and *Whirlwind*.

*Group VII*—Thornycroft 'W' Class

| name | builder | laid down | launched | completed |
|------|---------|-----------|----------|-----------|
| *Wolsey* | Thornycroft | 28 Mar '17 | 16 Mar '18 | 14 May '18 |
| *Woolston* | do. | 25 Apr '17 | 27 Jan '18 | 28 June '18 |

*Displacement*: 1,130 tons (standard).

*Dimensions*: As Group V.

*Machinery*: As Group V.

*Bunkers* and *Radius*: As Group V.

*Armament*: Guns as Group V; six 21-inch T.T. (2 × 3).

*Complement*: As Group V.

*Notes:* Once again Thornycrofts produced their characteristic version of the basic Admiralty design. Identical to their 'V' boats but armed with triple T.T. Both converted to 'Wairs' and served in World War II (see later notes).

*Group VIII*—Modified 'W' Class, 1st Group

| name | builder | laid down | launched | completed |
|------|---------|-----------|----------|-----------|
| *Vansittart* | Beardmore | 1 July '18 | 17 Apr '19 | 5 Nov '19 |
| *Vimy* (ex-*Vantage*)* | do. | 16 Sept '18 | *Cancelled September 1919* | |
| *Venomous* (ex-*Venom*)† | John Brown | 31 May '18 | 21 Dec '18 | June '19 |
| *Verity* | do. | 17 May '18 | 19 Mar '19 | 17 Sept '19 |
| *Volunteer* | Wm. Denny | 16 Apr '18 | 17 Apr '19 | 7 Nov '19 |
| *Votary* | do. | 18 June '18 | *Cancelled 12 April 1919* | |
| *Wanderer* | Fairfield | 7 Aug '18 | 1 May '19 | 18 Sept '19 |
| *Warren* | do. | ? | *Cancelled September 1919* | |
| *Welcome* | Hawthorn Leslie | 9 Apr '18 | *Cancelled 12 April 1919* | |
| *Welfare* | do. | 22 June '18 | *Cancelled 12 April 1919* | |
| *Whitehall* | Swan Hunter | June '18 | 11 Sept '19 | 9 July '24‡ |
| *Whitehead* | do. | ? | *Cancelled 12 April 1919* | |
| *Wren* | Yarrow | June '18 | 11 Nov '19 | 27 Jan '23§ |
| *Wye* | do. | Jan '18 | *Cancelled September 1919* | |

\* Renamed 16 August 1919.   † Renamed 24 April 1919.
‡ Completed by Chatham DY.   § Completed by Pembroke DY.

*Displacement*: 1,112 tons (standard), 1,505 tons (deep load).
*Dimensions*: As Groups IV and VI.
*Machinery*: Three Yarrow boilers, 250 lb/in$^2$; two shafts; independent reduction Brown-Curtis turbines (except Swan Hunter boats, Parsons); 27,000 S.H.P. = 34 knots, at 260 r.p.m.
*Bunkers* and *Radius*: 318–24 tons (normal), 374 tons (max); 3,210 miles @ 15 knots, 600 miles @ full speed.
*Armament*: Four 4·7-inch B.L. Mk I on CP VI* mountings, two 2-pounders; six 21-inch T.T. (2 × 3).
*Complement*: 134.
*Notes*: Although the dimensions were the same as the original Admiralty 'V' and 'W' boats, in this repeat order the hull-form was modified slightly, and the familiar concave stern was abandoned in favour of a straight stern. The change to the 4·7-inch gun was prompted by the general belief that the old 4-inch Mk V was inferior to the German 4·1-inch, and since the bigger gun had al-

ready been introduced in the leaders, it made little sense to cling to the 4-inch.

The margin of stability in the original design made the alteration possible, and so the Modified 'Ws' became the most powerful fleet destroyers in the world; despite the disadvantage of separate charges, the 4·7-inch loading mechanism was so simple that the weight of fire per minute was equal to the old 4-inch.

All ordered January 1918, but as the tables show, a number were suspended after the Armistice and finally cancelled.

*Appearance*: In general the class resembled the 'W' boats, but all had heavier funnel-caps. The shape and bulk of the 4·7-inch was distinctive, and lacked the familiar loading tray which projected to the rear of the 4-inch shield. At one stage between the Wars *Wanderer* had no shields to her guns, but minor variations such as these were only temporary.

*Group IX*—Modified 'W' Class, 2nd Group

| name | builder | laid down | launched | completed |
|------|---------|-----------|----------|-----------|
| *Vashon* | Beardmore | ? | *Cancelled 26 November 1918* | |
| *Vengeful* | do. | ? | *Cancelled 26 November 1918* | |
| *Veteran* | John Brown | 30 Aug '18 | 26 Apr '19 | 13 Nov '19 |
| *Vigo* | do. | Not begun | *Cancelled 26 November 1918* | |
| *Wistful* (ex-*Vigorous*)* | do. | ? | *Cancelled 26 November 1918* | |
| *Virulent* | do. | ? | *Cancelled 26 November 1918* | |
| *Volage* | do. | ? | *Cancelled 26 November 1918* | |
| *Volcano* | do. | ? | *Cancelled 26 November 1918* | |
| *Wager* | Wm. Denny | 2 Aug '18 | *Cancelled 12 April 1919* | |
| *Wake* | do. | 14 Oct '18 | *Cancelled 26 November 1918* | |
| *Waldegrave* | do. | Not begun | *Cancelled 26 November 1918* | |
| *Walton* | do. | Not begun | *Cancelled 26 November 1918* | |
| *Whitaker* | do. | Not begun | *Cancelled 26 November 1918* | |
| *Watson* | Fairfield | ? | *Cancelled September 1919* | |
| | (believed launched in 1919 to clear slip) | | | |
| *Wave* | do. | ? | *Cancelled December 1918* | |
| *Weasel* | do. | ? | *Cancelled 26 November 1918* | |
| *Whitebear* | do. | ? | *Cancelled 26 November 1918* | |
| *Wellesley* | Hawthorn Leslie | 30 Aug '18 | *Cancelled 26 November 1918* | |

*Group IX*—Modified 'W' Class, 2nd Group—*continued*

| name | builder | laid down | launched | completed |
|------|---------|-----------|----------|-----------|
| *Werewolf* | do. | 1918 | 17 July '19 | *Cancelled* |
| | | | | *12 April 1919* |
| *Westphal* | do. | ? | *Cancelled 12 April 1919* | |
| *Westward Ho!* | do. | ? | *Cancelled 12 April 1919* | |
| *Wheeler* | Scotts | July '18 | *Cancelled 12 April 1919* | |
| *Whip* | do. | ? | *Cancelled 26 November 1918* | |
| *Whippet* | do. | ? | *Cancelled 26 November 1918* | |
| *Whelp* | do. | ? | *Cancelled September 1919* | |
| *Whitshed* | Swan Hunter | 3 June '18 | 31 Jan '19 | 11 July '19 |
| *Wild Swan* | do. | July '18 | 17 May '19 | 14 Nov '19 |
| *Willoughby* | do. | ? | *Cancelled 12 April 1919* | |
| *Winter* | do. | ? | *Cancelled 26 November 1918* | |
| *Witherington* | J. S. White | 27 Sept '18 | 16 Apr. '19 | 10 Oct '19 |
| *Wivern* | do. | 19 Aug '18 | 16 Apr '19 | 23 Dec '19 |
| *Wolverine* | do. | 8 Oct '18 | 17 July '19 | 27 July '20 |
| *Worcester*† | do. | 20 Dec '18 | 24 Oct '19 | 20 Sept '22 |
| *Wrangler* | Yarrow | 3 Feb '19 | *Cancelled September 1919* | |
| *Yeoman* | do. | ? | *Cancelled 12 April 1919* | |
| *Zealous* | do. | ? | *Cancelled 12 April 1919* | |
| *Zebra* | do. | ? | *Cancelled 12 April 1919* | |
| *Zodiac* | do. | ? | *Cancelled 12 April 1919* | |

\* Renamed June 1918.    † Completed by Portsmouth Dockyard.

*Displacement*: As Group VIII.
*Dimensions*: As Group VIII.
*Machinery*: As Group VIII.
*Bunkers* and *Radius*: As Group VIII.
*Armament*: As Group VIII.
*Complement*: As Group VIII.
*Notes*: All ordered April 1918, and differed from the earlier Modified 'W' group in having the boilers rearranged; with the double boiler-room transposed the forefunnel became the thicker of the two.
*Appearance*: The reversed funnel arrangement made these boats distinctive, but in addition they differed from the other groups in having two single pom-poms mounted *en echelon* between the funnels.

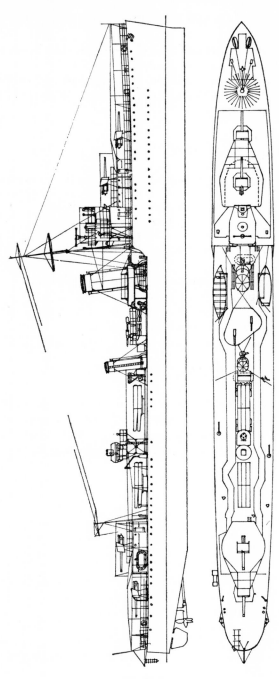

*Veteran* (Modified 'W' Class) as built

*Witherington* and *Wivern* had their after-funnels built in sideways, but this difference could not be easily spotted.

24 November 1918 material for *Whelp* transferred to Pembroke, material for *Watson* to Devonport, material for *Warren* to Chatham; boilers of *Vigo* to *Whelp*.

*Group X*—Thornycroft Modified 'W' Class

| name | builder | laid down | launched | completed |
|------|---------|-----------|----------|-----------|
| *Wishart* | Thornycroft | 18 May '18 | 18 July '19 | June '20 |
| *Witch** | do. | 13 June '18 | 11 Nov '19 | Mar '24 |

* Completed at Devonport Dockyard.

*Displacement*: 1,140 tons (standard), 1,550 tons (full load).

*Dimensions*: 300'(pp), 312'(oa) × 30' 7″ × 10' 11″.

*Machinery*: Three Thornycroft boilers; two shafts; Brown-Curtis all-geared turbines; 30,000 S.H.P. = 35 knots.

*Bunkers* and *Radius*: 322 tons (normal), 374 tons (max); 2,420 miles @ 12 knots.

*Armament*: As Groups VIII and IX.

*Complement*: 134.

*Notes*: These were the Thornycroft variations on the 2nd group of Modified 'Ws', but with higher freeboard and greater beam to incorporate more powerful machinery. With their tall, well-proportioned funnels they were the best-looking of the 'V & W' classes.

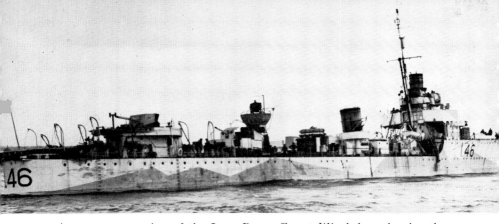

A stern quarter view of the Long Range Escort *Winchelsea*, showing the large number of depth charge throwers mounted aft.

The old destoyers had to retire one day: two melancholy views of 'V & Ws' laid up awaiting scrapping—*Verity* (above) at Barrow c. 1946, and *Wivern* (below), with another 'Modified W' and an ex-American flush-decker alongside, at Charlestown in the Firth of Forth, c. 1948.

(*Above*) The after part of *Wakeful* during fitting out at Clydebank, showing the torpedo tubes in the firing position and housed fore-and-aft.

(*Left*) The set of triple 21-inch torpedo tubes of *Wakeful*, c. 1920.

Two views of the standard 4-inch Q.F. Mark V which armed both 'V & W' class destroyers. The ship is probably the *Vehement*, fitting out at Denny's yard, Dumbarton, late in 1917.

*Venomous* fitting out at Clydebank in May 1919, showing both sets of torpedo tubes and 'X' and 'Y' 4·7-inch guns. Note the straight stern which characterized the 'Modified Ws'.

Australian *Stuart* as she appeared between the wars as leader to the R.A.N. force of four 'V & W' boats.

Two views of *Stuart* as she appeared in 1945, acting as a fast transport between Australia and New Guinea. It is not clear if a 'Hedgehog' has been added in 'A' position, but only 'B' and 'X' 4·7-inch guns remain, with a pair of 2-pdr. pom-poms between the funnels, all torpedo tubes removed, and 20-mm guns in the bridge wings and on the quarterdeck.

The former 'V-leader' *Vampire* as she appeared in the Australian Navy pre-war. Note that the original recognition feature, the compass platform before the searchlight, remained unaltered.

Australian *Waterhen*, otherwise known as the 'Chook', as she appeared pre-war. Note that she carries paravanes on the quarterdeck, slung on patent luffing davits.

Two views of the *Vendetta*, the only 'V & W' of the 'Scrapiron Flotilla' to survive the Second World War, pre-war (above) and in 1945 (overleaf). Note that she still has her old range finder, three torpedo tubes, and a 12-pdr. in place of the old pom-pom abaft the funnel.

## FATES OF VESSELS NOT IN SERVICE SEPTEMBER 1939

*Vehement*  Mined 1 August 1918 in North Sea, and wreck sunk by gunfire next day.

*Vittoria*  Torpedoed by Russian submarine *Pantera* in Baltic 1 September 1919 (some sources claim her sunk by a Russian M.T.B.).

*Verulam*  Sunk by Russian mine in Baltic 4 September 1919 (wreck may have been salvaged by Finnish government subsequently).

*Valhalla*  Sold to J. Cashmore, Newport (Mon.) 17 December 1931 and BU 1932.

*Valkyrie*  Handed over to Ward 24 August 1936 in part payment for S.S. *Majestic*, and BU at Inverkeithing.

*Vectis*  Handed over to Ward 25 August 1936 in part payment for S.S. *Majestic*, and BU at Inverkeithing.

*Venturous*
*Shakespeare*  Handed over to Ward 2 September 1936 in part payment for S.S. *Majestic*, and BU at Inverkeithing.

*Spenser*  Handed over to Ward 29 September 1936 in part payment for S.S. *Majestic* and BU at Inverkeithing.

*Violent*  Handed over to Ward 8 March 1937 in part payment for S.S. *Majestic* and BU at Inverkeithing.

*Bruce*  Disarmed 1938 for service as a target; sunk during torpedo trials off Isle of Wight 22 November 1939.

## *1938–1945 ALTERATIONS, ETC.*

'*Wair*' *Escort Conversions*
*One ex-Group II*

| name | where converted | from | to |
|---|---|---|---|
| *Wallace* | Devonport Dockyard | Oct '38 | June '39 |

*Displacement and Dimensions*: as Group II (draught 8′ 6″(fwd), 10′ 3″(aft).
*Machinery*: Unaltered.
*Bunkers* and *Radius*: 409 tons (max); 1,790 miles @ 12 knots.
*Armament*: (1939) Four 4-inch A.A. Mk XVI (2 × 2), four 2-pounders A.A. (1 × 4), eight ·5-inch MGs (2 × 4).
(1942) Two 20-mm. Oerlikon A.A. (2 × 1) added in wings of bridge.
(1944) Four 4-inch A.A., six 2-pounders A.A. (1 × 4, 2 × 1), four 20-mm. A.A. (4 × 1).
*A/S Weapons*: Four depth-charge throwers.
*Complement*: 187.
*Notes*: The only leader converted under the 1938 'Wair' programme, she differed from the remainder in having a multiple pom-pom. A single Oerlikon was added in each bridge-wing by 1942, and by 1944 Oerlikons had replaced the quadruple machine-guns as well. Two additional single 2-pounder A.A. had been sited abreast of the funnels.

*Two ex-Group I, five ex-Group IV, one ex-Group V, four ex-Group VI, two ex-Group VII*

| name | where converted | from | to |
|---|---|---|---|
| *Whitley* | Chatham Dockyard | Mar '38 | Oct '38 |
| *Wolsey* | Malta Dockyard | Sept '38 | Dec '39 |
| *Valorous* | Chatham Dockyard | Nov '38 | 1 June '39 |
| *Vivien* | do. | Dec '38 | 25 Oct '39 |
| *Winchester* | Portsmouth Dockyard | Apr '39 | 5/9 Apr '40 |
| *Valentine* | Devonport Dockyard | June '39 | 23 Apr '40 |
| *Woolston* | Chatham Dockyard | May '39 | 9 Oct '39 |
| *Vega* | do. | May '39 | 27 Nov '39 |
| *Vimiera* | Portsmouth Dockyard | June '39 | 8 Jan '40 |
| *Wryneck* | Gibraltar Dockyard | Sept '39 | Apr '40 |

| name | where converted | from | to |
|------|-----------------|------|-----|
| *Verdun* | Chatham Dockyard | Sept '39 | 11 July '40 |
| *Westminster* | Devonport Dockyard | June '39 | 8 Jan '40 |
| *Vanity* | Rosyth Dockyard | Oct '39 | 12 Aug '40 |
| *Viceroy* | Portsmouth Dockyard | May '40 | 10 Jan '41 |
| *Wolfhound* | Chatham Dockyard | ? '39 | 2 May '40 |

*Displacement* and *Dimensions*: As originally built.

*Machinery*: Unaltered.

*Bunkers* and *Radius*: 330 tons (max, except Thornycroft boats, 336 tons); 2,150 miles @ 12 knots (Thornycroft boats 2,190 miles).

*Armament*: (1939–40) Four-inch A.A. Mk XVI (2 × 2), eight ·5-inch MGs (2 × 4).

(1941-42) single 20-mm. Oerlikon A.A. added in each bridge-wing, and single 20-mm. replaced ·5-inch MGs in most, if not all.

*Notes*: Four more conversions authorized, but *Walrus* lost 1938, and *Wakeful*, *Windsor* and *Wrestler* not taken in hand. *Wolfhound* was attacked by dive-bombers off East Coast on 3 September 1941, and broke in half when bracketed by bombs. The stern half was towed into port, and she was rebuilt at Chatham between November 1941 and April 1943.


*Unconverted Destroyers*, Groups IV, VI and VIII

| name | fate |
|------|------|
| *Vampire* (R.A.N.) | Sunk by Japanese aircraft 1942 |
| *Vendetta* (R.A.N.) | |
| *Venetia* | Mined 1940 |
| *Vortigern* | Torpedoed by E-boat 1942 |
| *Voyager* (R.A.N.) | Bombed by Japanese aircraft and beached 1942 |
| *Wakeful* | Torpedoed by E-boat 1940. |
| *Waterhen* (R.A.N.) | Sunk by Italian and German aircraft 1941 |
| *Wessex* | Sunk by aircraft 1940. |
| *Whirlwind* | Torpedoed 1940 |
| *Wren* | Sunk by aircraft 1940 |

*Notes*: These vessels all remained more or less in their pre-war state, either due to their early loss or their employment in distant waters

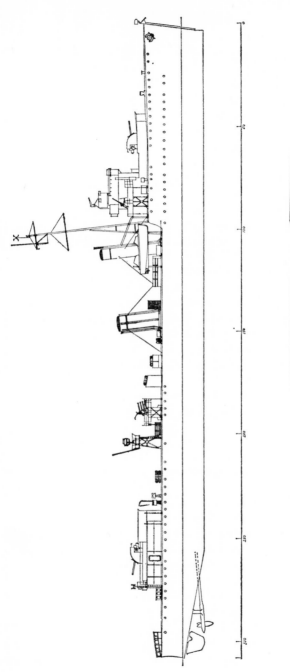

*Vanity* after conversion to 'Wair' A.A. escort vessel

(the four R.A.N. boats). Where alterations were carried out they were restricted to reducing torpedo-armament in favour of A.A. weapons. Individual ships had a wide range of weapons such as Lewis guns, while some of the R.A.N. destroyers used captured Italian machine-guns.

*Short Range Escorts*

| name | armament |
| --- | --- |
| *Broke* | Two 4·7-inch, one 3-inch A.A., six 21-inch T.T., five 20-mm. A.A., one 'Hedgehog' ATW, DCs. |
| *Campbell* | Three 4·7-inch (A, B & Y positions), one 4-inch A.A. (X position), two 2-pounders (between funnels), two 20-mm. A.A., six 21-inch T.T., etc. |
| *Douglas* | Two 4·7-inch (B & X), one 3-inch A.A., three 21-inch T.T., etc. |
| *Keppel* | Two 4·7-inch (B & X), one 3-inch A.A., four 20-mm. A.A., six 21-inch T.T., one 'Hedgehog' ATW, etc. |
| *Mackay* | Four 4·7-inch, one 3-inch A.A., six 21-inch T.T., etc. |
| *Montrose* | Two 4·7-inch, two 6-pounders (1 × 2), one 3-inch A.A., etc. |
| *Stuart* (R.A.N.) (1944–45) | Two 4·7-inch, one 3-inch A.A., two 2-pounders (between funnels), two 20-mm. A.A. (bridge-wings), T.T. removed. |
| *Whitshed, Witherington* and *Wivern* | Two 4·7-inch, two 6-pounders (1 × 2), six 21-inch T.T. (no T.T. in *Witherington*), two/six 20-mm. A.A., etc. |
| *Malcolm, Veteran* and *Wolverine* | Two 4·7-inch, one 12-pounder A.A., three 21-inch T.T., one 'Hedgehog' ATW, etc. |
| *Windsor* and *Walpole* | Two 4-inch, two 6-pounders (1 × 2), three 2-pounder (3 × 1), two 20-mm. A.A., etc. |
| *Wishart* and *Witch* | Two or three 4·7-inch, one 12-pounder A.A., no T.T. |

*Short Range Escorts—continued*

| name | armament |
|------|----------|
| *Worcester* | Four 4·7-inch, one 12-pounder A.A., two 2-pounder A.A., two 20-mm. A.A., three 21-inch T.T. |
| *Vivacious* | Three 4-inch, one 12-pounder A.A., etc., as *Worcester*. |

*Bunkers* and *Endurance*: 365 tons (leaders 490 tons); 2,380/2,940 miles @ 12 knots.

*Notes*: By 1942 all the remaining unaltered destroyers which were exclusively employed on escort duties were classed as Short Range Escorts (S.R.E.s). They included all the surviving old leaders and most of the Modified 'Ws'. None of the Group IX or X Modified 'W' type were suitable for conversion to Long Range Escorts, due to the double boiler-room being forward instead of aft.

Being low on endurance these vessels were mainly restricted to Mediterranean and East Coast escort work, but for all that they ranged as far afield as West Africa, and accounted for nearly a third of all the submarines sunk by the class as a whole. Those ships likely to see surface action, such as *Keppel* on the North Russian route, retained their full complement of torpedo-tubes. Six employed on the East Coast were fitted in 1944 with a rapid-fire twin 6-pounder mounting for use against E-boats.

*Appearance*: *Broke* underwent a refit at the beginning of the war, which resulted in her forecastle being extended farther aft, and her fore-funnel being replaced by a thin round one. Although no conclusive evidence has been discovered, there is reason to believe that she had a partial conversion to improve her endurance, which probably involved the removal of one of her four boilers.

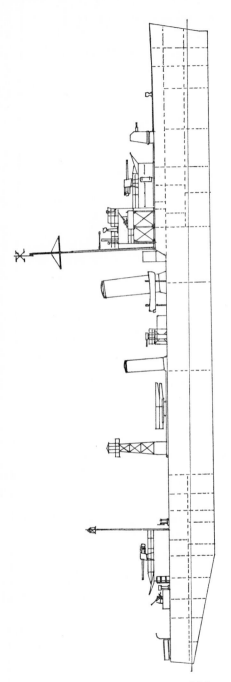
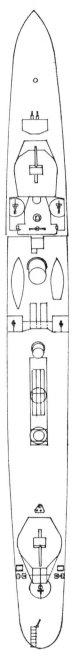

*Wivern, etc.* as modified for East Coast convoy escort duties with twin 6-pdrs. forward

## *Long Range Escort Conversions,* ex-Groups IV, V, VI and VIII

| name | where converted | from | to |
|------|-----------------|------|-----|
| *Vimy* | Portsmouth Dockyard | Jan '41 | June '41 |
| *Viscount* | Liverpool | June '41 | Dec '41 |
| *Vanessa* | Green and Silley Weir, Blackwall | Aug '41 | June '42 |
| *Winchelsea* | Sheerness Dockyard | Jan '42 | Apr '42 |
| *Venomous* | Clyde | Jan '42 | Aug '42 |
| *Whitehall* | Sheerness Dockyard | May '42 | Aug '42 |
| *Volunteer* | Rosyth Dockyard | Aug '42 | Jan '43 |
| *Vidette* | Sheerness Dockyard | Sept '42 | Jan '43 |
| *Vanquisher* | Portsmouth Dockyard | Sept '42 | Apr '43 |
| *Vesper* | Chatham Dockyard | Dec '42 | Sept '43 |
| *Walker* | Thames | Jan '43 | May '43 |
| *Wrestler* | Sheerness Dockyard | Jan '43 | May '43 |
| *Warwick* | Dundee | Jan '43 | May '43 |
| *Wanderer* | Devenport Dockyard | Jan '43 | May '43 |
| *Vansittart* | Middlesbrough | Jan '43 | June '43 |
| *Versatile* | Grangemouth | Jan '43 | Sept '43 |
| *Verity* | Portsmouth Dockyard | Apr '43 | Oct '43 |
| *Vanoc* | Thornycroft, Southampton | Apr '43 | Nov '43 |
| *Watchman* | Liverpool | Apr '43 | Aug '43 |
| *Velox* | Sheerness Dockyard | Dec '43 | May '44 |

*Displacement, Dimensions,* etc.: As Short Range Escorts, etc.

*Machinery*: As built, but only two boilers; 18,000 S.H.P. = 24½ knots.

*Bunkers* and *Radius*: 450 tons (*Viscount* 455 tons) O.F.; 2,930 miles @ 12 knots.

*Armament*: Two/three 4-inch or 4·7-inch, two/three 2-pounders A.A., four/five 20-mm. A.A. guns; three 21-inch T.T. in some.

*Notes*: This conversion involved the removal of the forward boiler, and converting the boiler-room to a fuel tank, to provide additional endurance for North Atlantic convoy escort work. The reduced speed was still adequate, and the opportunity was taken to overhaul armament and habitability. The increased endurance put the L.R.E.s or 'long-leggers' on a par with the new frigates in being able to accompany a convoy all the way across the Atlantic without refuelling.

APPENDICES

*Appearance*: All changes stemmed from the removal of the boiler and changes to armament; i.e. the forefunnel was removed, the new anti-submarine weapon 'Hedgehog' was installed in place of 'A' gun, and the armament of 20-mm. Oerlikon guns was augmented. In addition, less obvious changes were made to the R.D.F. (radar) installation. As no two were alike, photographs were the only accurate guide to individual variations of armament and equipment. *Vanessa* and *Venomous* were Flying Training Targets by February 1944; all anti-submarine weapons were removed, and stowage for recovered practice torpedoes was provided between the funnel and after superstructure. Some, such as *Watchman*, had a 2-pounder pom-pom (single) added on the forecastle; others shipped a fifth Oerlikon gun on the quarterdeck, or retained 'A' gun.

The *Velox* presents something of a mystery; the only refit long enough for a conversion to a Long Range Escort is the one listed, yet various authorities differ over the question of whether she was converted or not. As there is a photograph of her with only one funnel, taken in May 1944, the answer seems to be that she underwent a refit to convert to L.R.E., but for one reason or another was never used on North Atlantic escort duties, and was allocated immediately as a Flying Training Target Ship (see *Vanessa* and *Venomous* above). The most likely reason would be some major fault developing in her machinery, which would made her unreliable for sea-service, but not unsuitable for subsidiary work.

Another mystery is the proposed conversion of *Keppel* to L.R.E. The author is unable to trace any photographic or other firm evidence such as a lengthy refit, to justify this, yet the standard authority, Edgar J. March, says she was converted, and some Admiralty returns confirm this. However, this may only have been an 'approval' which was never carried out. If it had been, she would have stowed 580 tons of fuel, giving her an endurance of 2,540 miles @ 12 knots.

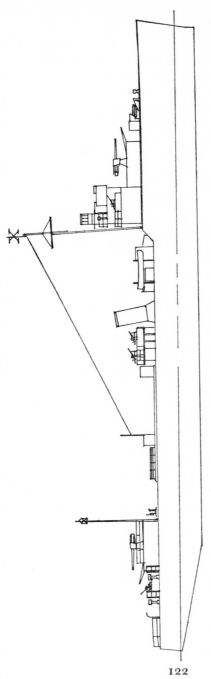

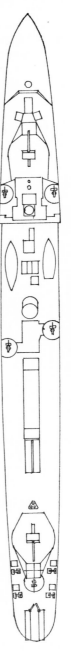

Long Range Escort

APPENDICES

# FATES OF VESSELS IN SERVICE IN SEPTEMBER 1939

**Valentine** Beached or abandoned 15 May 1940 in the Scheldt Estuary after heavy air attack; wreck salvaged and BU in Belgium, January 1953

**Whitley** Beached 19 May 1940 between Nieuport and Ostend after heavy air attack

**Wessex** Sunk 24 May 1940 by air attack off Calais

**Wakeful** Torpedoed 29 May 1940 off Nieuport by German MTB *S.30* while evacuating troops from Dunkirk

**Whirlwind** Torpedoed 5 July 1940 by *U.34* SW of Ireland

**Wren** Sunk 27 July 1940 by German aircraft off Aldeburgh

**Venetia** Mined 19 October 1940 in Thames Estuary

**Wryneck** Sunk 27 April 1941 by air attack South of Morea, during evacuation of Greece

**Waterhen** Sunk 30 June 1941 off Sollum, Eastern Mediterranean after heavy bomb damage the previous day

**Vimiera** Mined 9 January 1942 off Nore

**Vortigern** Torpedoed 15 March 1942 by E-boat off Cromer

**Vampire** Sunk 9 April 1942 by Japanese aircraft in Bay of Bengal

**Wild Swan** Bombed 17 June 1942 by German aircraft in Bay of Biscay, and sank after collision with Spanish trawler

**Voyager** Beached on Timor in Pacific 23 September 1942 and destroyed by her crew, following heavy damage by Japanese aircraft

**Veteran** Torpedoed 26 September 1942 by *U.404* in North Atlantic

**Broke** Heavily damaged by gunfire from shore batteries at Algiers 8 November 1942 and sank in tow next day

**Warwick** Torpedoed 20 February 1944 off Trevose Head, Cornwall, by *U.413*

**Wrestler** Mined 6 June 1944 off Normandy and damaged beyond repair; sold 20 July 1944 to Cashmore and arrived at Newport, Mon., for BU 15 August 1944

**Montrose** Damaged in collision with American LST off Arromanches 10 June 1944; towed to Immingham and paid off; sold 31 January 1946 (with **Wanderer**) to B.I.S. Corp. and allocated to Hughes Bolckow; BU completed by April 1946

**Walpole** Mined 6 January 1945 in North Sea and not repaired; sold 8 February 1945 and BU by T. W. Ward at Grays by September 1946

**Wallace** and **Viscount** Sold 20 March 1945 to B.I.S. Corp. and allocated to Clayton & Davie, Dunston; **Viscount** arrived 27 May 1947 and both BU by September 1947

**Douglas, Wishart** and **Winchelsea** Sold 20 March 1945 to B.I.S. Corp. and allocated to T. W. Ward; **Douglas** BU at Inverkeithing May 1945–September 1946, **Winchelsea** completed BU at Rosyth by 31 December 1945, and **Wishart** likewise at Inverkeithing

**Watchman** Sold 23 July 1945 to B.I.S. Corp. and BU by Ward at Inverkeithing

**Keppel** and **Malcolm** Sold to B.I.S. Corp. 25 July 1945, allocated to Ward and BU at Barrow

**Vanoc** Sold 26 July 1945 to B.I.S. Corp. and allocated to Wards, but wrecked off Penryn in June 1946 while in tow; later salvaged and BU at Falmouth by Wards, by November 1947

**Whitehall** Sold October 1945 to B.I.S. Corp. and BU by Wards at Barrow from 27 October 1945 to 30 December 1948

**Westcott** Sold 8 January 1946 to B.I.S. Corp. and BU at Troon by Arnott Young

**Wolverine** Sold 28 January 1946 and BU as **Westcott**

**Wanderer** Sold 31 January 1946 (with **Montrose**) to B.I.S. Corp. and allocated to Hughes Bolckow; BU completed by July 1946

**Vansittart** Sold 25 February 1946 to B.I.S. Corp. and BU by Cashmore at Newport May 1946 to May 1947

**Winchester** Sold 5 March 1946 to B.I.S. Corp. and BU by T.W. Ward at Inverkeithing

**Walker** Sold 15 March 1946 and BU at Troon by Arnott Young (completed by May 1947)

**Witch** Sold 12 July 1946 and BU by Brechin at Granton by January 1948

**Worcester** Mined 23 December 1943 and laid up; renamed **Yeoman** in June 1945 as an accommodation ship; sold 17 September 1946 to B.I.S. Corp. and BU at Grays by February 1947

**Velox** and **Wivern** Sold 18 February 1947 to B.I.S. Corp. and BU at Rosyth by Metal Industries by May and December 1948 respectively

**Campbell, Mackay, Vivien, Whitshed** and **Woolston** All sold 18 February 1947 to B.I.S. Corp. and allocated as follows:

**Campbell**—BU by Metal Industries, Rosyth February to October 1948

**Mackay**—BU at Charlestown February 1949 to February 1950 by Metal Industries

**Vivien**—BU at Charlestown by Metal Industries by May 1948

**Whitshed**—BU at Gateshead by J. J. King by February 1949

**Woolston**—BU at Grangemouth by G. W. Brunton by September 1948

**Stuart** Sold Feburary 1947 to T. Carr & Co., and BU in Australia

**Valorous, Vanessa, Vanity, Vanquisher, Vega, Venomous, Verity, Vesper, Vidette, Vivacious, Volunteer, Westminster, Windsor** and **Wolsey** All sold to B.I.S. Corp. 4 March 1947 and allocated as follows:

**Valorous**—BU at Thornaby by Stockton Shipping and Salvage Co.

**Vanessa**—Arrived at Charlestown for BU by Metal Industries, February 1948

**Vidette** and **Vanity**—BU by Brunton completed at Grangemouth by April 1949

**Vanquisher**—BU at Charlestown by Metal Industries December 1948 to June 1949

**Vega**—BU by Clayton & Davie at Dunston 26 March to 30 October 1948

**Venomous**—BU at Rosyth August to November 1948

**Vesper**—BU by Ward at Inverkeithing by December 1949

**Vivacious**—BU at Charlestown by Metal Industries October 1948 to March 1949

**Volunteer**—BU by Brechin at Granton from April 1948 to 31 January 1949

**Westminster**—BU by Metal Industries at Charlestown August to 31 December 1948

**Windsor**—BU at Charlestown May 1949 to January 1950

**Wolsey**—BU at Sunderland by Young by May 1949

**Witherington** Sold 20 March 1947 to B.I.S. Corp. and allocated to Metal Industries, but wrecked 29 April 1947 *en route* to Charlestown

**Wolfhound** Sold 18 February 1948 and BU at Granton by Brechin completed by January 1949

**Vendetta** Discarded 1945 and scuttled off Sydney Heads 2 July 1948

**Vimy** Sold to B.I.S. Corp. (date unknown) and BU at Rosyth February to July 1948

**Viceroy** As **Vimy**, but BU by Brechin, Granton, June 1948 to August 1949

**Versatile** Sold 1948 to B.I.S. Corp. and BU at Granton by Brechin January to December 1949

**Verdun** Sold to B.I.S. Corp. (date unknown) and BU by Brechin, Granton, 1946–47

# LIST OF U-BOATS AND ITALIAN SUBMARINES SUNK BY 'V & W' DESTROYERS AND LEADERS

| date | sinking | vessels involved; location |
|---|---|---|
| 27 July '18 | *UB.107* | *Vanessa*; off Scarborough |
| 30 Jan '40 | *U.55* | *Whitshed, Fowey* and a/c of 228 Sqn, R.A.F.; 100 miles W Ushant |
| 30 Sept '40 | *Gondar* | *Stuart, Diamond*; NW Alexandria |
| 11 Oct '40 | *Durbo* | *Wrestler, Firedrake*; off Gibraltar |
| 8 Mar '41 | *U.47/U.70* | *Wolverine*; S Iceland (see Note) |
| 17 Mar '41 | *U.99* | *Walker*; W Hebrides |
| 17 Mar '41 | *U.100* | *Walker, Vanoc*; W Hebrides |
| 5 Apr '41 | *U.76* | *Wolverine, Scarborough*; S Iceland |
| 2 June '41 | *U.147* | *Wanderer, Periwinkle*; NW Ireland |
| 27 June '41 | *Glauco* | *Wishart*; off Gibraltar |
| 29 June '41 | *U.651* | *Malcolm, Scimitar, Speedwell, Arabis* and *Violet*; S Iceland |
| 3 Aug '41 | *U.401* | *Wanderer, St. Albans* and *Hydrangea*; SW Ireland |
| 11 Sept '41 | *U.207* | *Veteran* and *Leamington*; Denmark Strait |
| 21 Sept '41 | *Alessandro Malaspina* | *Vimy*; off Gibraltar |
| 2 Feb. '42 | *U.581* | *Westcott*; SW Azores |
| 27 Mar '42 | *U.587* | *Volunteer, Leamington, Aldenham* and *Grove*; SW Ireland |
| 2 May '42 | *U.74* | *Wishart, Wrestler* and a/c of 202 Sqn, R.A.F.; SE Valencia |
| 12 May '42 | *Dagabur* | *Wolverine*; off Balearic Is. |
| 3 Sept '42 | *U.162* | *Vimy, Pathfinder* and *Quentin*; NE Trinidad |
| 15 Oct '42 | *U.619* | *Viscount*; N Atlantic |
| 15 Nov '42 | *U.411* | *Wrestler*; off Bone |
| 26 Dec '42 | *U.357* | *Vanessa* and *Hesperus*; NW Rockall |
| 4 Feb '43 | *U.187* | *Vimy* and *Beverley*; 600 miles SE Cape Farewell |
| 17 Feb '43 | *U.69* | *Viscount*; N Atlantic |
| 6 May '43 | *U.125* | *Vidette*; ESE Newfoundland |
| 23 Oct '43 | *U.274* | *Vidette, Duncan* and a/c of 224 Sqn, R.A.F.; SE Iceland |

| date | sinking | vessels involved; location |
|---|---|---|
| 29 Oct '43 | U.282 | *Vidette, Duncan* and *Sunflower*; North Atlantic |
| 31 Oct '43 | U.306 | *Whitehall* and *Geranium*; NE Azores |
| 31 Oct '43 | U.732 | *Douglas* and trawler *Imperialist*; off Tangier |
| 1 Nov '43 | U.340 | *Witherington, Active, Fleetwood* and a/c of 179 Sqn, R.A.F.; off Tangier |
| 17 Jan '44 | U.305 | *Wanderer* and *Glenarm*; WSW Ireland |
| 30 Jan '44 | U.314 | *Whitehall* and *Meteor*; Barents Sea |
| 24 Feb '44 | U.713 | *Keppel*; off Narvik |
| 24 Feb '44 | U.761 | *Wishart, Anthony*, and a/c of 202 Sqn, R.A.F., VPO3 and VB127 Sqns, U.S.N. |
| 16 Mar '44 | U.392 | *Vanoc, Affleck* and a/c of VP63 Sqn, U.S.N. |
| 2 Apr '44 | U.360 | *Keppel*; off Hammerfest |
| 5 July '44 | U.390 | *Wanderer* and *Tavy*; Seine Bay |
| 20 Aug '44 | U.413 | *Vidette, Forester* and *Wensleydale*; S Brighton |
| 24 Aug '44 | U.354 | *Keppel, Mermaid, Peacock* and *Loch Dunvegan*; NE North Cape |
| 2 Sept '44 | U.394 | *Keppel, Whitehall, Mermaid, Peacock* and a/c of 825 Sqn from *Vindex*; off Jan Mayen Island |
| 6 Apr '44 | U.1195 | *Watchman*; SE Isle of Wight |
| 14 Mar '45 | U.714 | *Wivern* and *Natal*; off Berwick |
| 10 Apr '45 | U.878 | *Vanquisher* and *Tintagel Castle*; S Iceland |
| 16 Apr '45 | U.1274 | *Viceroy*; E Sunderland |

ADDITIONAL NOTES ON SUBMARINE LOSSES

As mentioned in Chapter 5 the list of submarine losses does not tally with the official list, as *U.714* has been attributed to *Wivern* as well as S.A.N.F. *Natal*. Furthermore, there is some dispute over *Wolverine*'s claim to have sunk *U.47* (Gunther Prien) in March 1941. *U.S. Submarine Losses, World War II*, has a footnote on p. 159 to the effect that *U.47* has been credited to the corvettes *Camellia* and *Arbutus*, and that the U-boat sunk by *Wolverine* was in fact *U.70*. This has been supported by recent British research.

# PENDANT LISTS AND PENDANT NUMBERS

*Note*: The position regarding destroyers' pendant numbers during 1914–18 remains obscure, despite the discovery of long-sought pendant lists which were thought to have been destroyed. Briefly, in 1914 all existing destroyers were identified by flying a 'flag superior' followed by a numeral; owing to the large numbers of destroyers there were two series, 'D' and 'H', although some older vessels in the so-called 'patrol flotillas' were given flag superior 'P'. These numbers were not painted up on the ship herself, but in 1914 the class letter was painted up, and there is evidence to suggest some random numbering at that time; however, this did not affect more than a few ships. Although some evidence suggests that pendant numbers were not uniformly painted up until September 1916, the order went out in *1915*, and some destroyers had numbers at Jutland.

After the outbreak of war distinguishing letters were dropped, and fresh pendant lists were prepared for the Grand Fleet flotillas. Initially flag superior 'F' was chosen, but as production of fleet destroyers was stepped up, flag superior 'G' was also made available, still for Grand Fleet destroyers. From 1917 the system began to break down as fleet destroyers were detached for convoy and patrol duty, until finally in 1920 the whole pendant list was simplified and reduced to flag superior 'D' with a few 'H' numbers.

Two points should be noted: leaders did not generally have their pendant numbers painted up (although exceptions were made to this rule) and minelayers changed their pendant numbers more frequently in order to confuse the enemy. An interesting point about the 'F' and 'G' lists is that the numerical order usually tallied with the flotilla's alphabetical order, following the leader's name. In other words, if *F.20* was allocated to the leader of the newly formed 30th Flotilla, *F.21* to *F.28* would belong to the destroyers of her division, and *F.29* to *F.37* would go to the divisional leader and her eight boats in alphabetical order.

FLAG SUPERIOR 'F'

| no. | ship | period used |
|-----|------|-------------|
| *F.A0* | *Vectis* | |
| *F.A1* | *Violent* | Aug. 1917 |
| *F.A2* | *Verulam* | et seq. |
| *F.A3* | *Vendetta* | |

| no. | ship | period used |
|---|---|---|
| F.A6 | Mackay | May–Oct. 1919 |
| F.A7 | Whitshed | while building to Nov. 1919 |
| F.0A | Spenser | Aug. 1917 |
| F.1A | Vehement | |
| ,, | Vanoc | late 1917 |
| F.2A | Verdun | Aug. 1917 |
| F.3A | Vanquisher | |
| F.4A | Vega | |
| F.5A | Vehement | late 1917 |
| F.8A | Vanoc | Aug. 1917 |
| F.9A | Valhalla | |
| ,, | Venetia | Aug. 1917 (later than Valhalla) |
| F.02 | Westminster | Mar.–Sept. 1918 |
| F.03 | Westcott | |
| F.05 | Valkyrie | |
| F.06 | Vectis | Mar.–June 1918 |
| F.07 | Vidette | June–Sept. 1918 |
| F.08 | Vanquisher | Jan.–June 1918 |
| ,, | Woolston | June 1918–Sept. 1919 |
| F.09 | Vega | Mar. 1918–Sept. 1919 |
| F.12 | Vehement | June–Aug. 1918 |
| ,, | Windsor | Sept. 1918–Sept. 1919 |
| F.14 | Venetia | Mar. 1918–Sĕt. 1919 |
| ,, | Keppel | Sept. 1919–1925 (while building) |
| F.15 | Walpole | Sept. 1918–Sept. 1919 |
| F.16 | Verdun | Mar. 1918–Sept. 1919 |
| F.18 | Wolfhound | |
| F.19 | Verulam | |
| F.20 | Whitley | post-Sept. 1918–Sept. 1919 |
| ,, | Stuart | Sept. 1919–1920 |
| F.21 | Vanquisher | reported late 1917 (uncertain) |
| ,, | Venturous | Jan.–Sept. 1918 |
| F.27 | Vanoc | Jan.–June 1918 |
| F.28 | Vesper | Oct. 1917 |
| ,, | Vimiera | Jan.–Sept. 1918 |
| F.29 | Versatile | Oct. 1917 |
| ,, | Vendetta | Jan. 1918–Sept. 1919 |
| F.30 | Venturous | Oct. 1917 |

| no. | ship | period used |
|---|---|---|
| „ | *Valentine* | Jan. 1918–Sept. 1919 |
| „ | *Montrose* | Sept. 1919–1920 |
| *F.31* | *Vittoria* | Oct. 1917 |
| „ | *Violent* | Mar. 1918–Oct. 1919 |
| *F.32* | *Vancouver* | Oct. 1917 |
| „ | *Wessex* | June 1918–Sept. 1919 |
| *F.33* | *Vivacious* | ⎫ |
| *F.34* | *Velox* | ⎬ Oct. 1917 |
| *F.35* | *Vortigern* | ⎭ |
| *F.36* | *Verity* | post Mar. 1918–Oct. 1919 |
| *F.37* | *Wakeful* | Jan. 1918–Sept. 1919 |
| *F.38* | *Viceroy* | ⎫ |
| *F.39* | *Vesper* | ⎬ Mar. 1918–Sept. 1919 |
| *F.40* | *Winchelsea* | ⎭ |
| „ | *Bruce* | Sept.–Oct. 1919 |
| *F.45* | *Montrose* | post Sept. 1918–Sept. 1919 |
| *F.48* | *Bruce* | June 1918–Sept. 1919 |
| *F.50* | *Douglas* | Sept. 1919–1920 |
| *F.51* | *Venturous* | ⎫ Nov. 1919–1920 |
| *F.52* | *Verdun* | ⎭ |
| *F.53* | *Volunteer* | Sept. 1919–1920 |
| *F.54* | *Versatile* | Uncertain, but changed by 1920 |
| *F.55* | *Walker* | ⎫ |
| *F.56* | *Whirlwind* | ⎬ |
| *F.57* | *Wrestler* | Nov. 1919–1920 |
| *F.58* | *Valkyrie* | ⎭ |
| *F.59* | *Wakeful* | Doubtful |
| *F.61* | *Vanoc* | Sept. 1919–1920 |
| *F.62* | *Vanquisher* | ⎫ Sept.–Oct. 1919 |
| *F.63* | *Venturous* | ⎭ |
| *F.64* | *Vittoria* | Sept. 1919 (already sunk) |
| *F.83* | *Valkyrie* | Nov. 1919–1920 |
| *F.84* | *Vanquisher* | 1917 (uncertain) |
| „ | *Vanoc* | Sept. 1918–Sept. 1919 |
| *F.85* | *Vanquisher* | Sept. 1918–Sept. 1919 |
| *F.86* | *Vehement* | Sept. 1918 (already sunk) |
| *F.87* | *Venturous* | Sept. 1918–Sept. 1919 |

| no. | ship | period used |
|---|---|---|
| F.89 | Shakespeare | Jan. 1918–Sept. 1919 |
| F.90 | Spenser | |
| F.91 | Verdun | Jan.–Mar. 1918 |
| F.92 | Valorous | Apr. 1917 |
| ,, | Vega | |
| F.93 | Venetia | Jan.–Mar. 1918 |
| F.94 | Vectis | |
| F.95 | Violent | |
| F.96 | Vittoria | late 1917 (uncertain) |
| ,, | Verulam | Jan.–Mar. 1918 |
| F.98 | Scott | |
| F.99 | Valentine | late 1917 (uncertain) |
| ,, | Viceroy | Jan.–Mar. 1918 |
| ,, | Winchester | Nov. 1919–1920 |
| ,, | Viscount | 1920 (uncertain) |

FLAG SUPERIOR 'G'

| no. | ship | period used |
|---|---|---|
| GA.5 | Wren | These numbers were allotted during building, but all four were given 'D' numbers before completion |
| GA.6 | Witch | |
| GA.7 | Whitehall | |
| GA.8 | Worcester | |
| G.9A | Valhalla | Nov. 1919–1920 |
| G.00 | Douglas | post Nov. 1918 |
| G.01 | Vivacious | Mar. 1918–Sept. 1919 |
| G.03 | Vortigern | |
| G.04 | Vancouver | |
| G.05 | Vittoria | |
| ,, | Wryneck | shown as post Sept. 1918, but *Vittoria* was not sunk until Sept. 1919 this may have been an erroneous entry |
| G.06 | Viscount | Sept. 1918–Sept. 1919 |
| G.08 | Walker | |
| G.09 | Watchman | Mar. 1918–Sept. 1919 |
| G.10 | Versatile | |
| G.16 | Voyager | Sept. 1918–Sept. 1919 |

FLAG SUPERIOR 'G'—*continued*

| no. | ship | period used |
|---|---|---|
| G.17 | Walrus | Mar. 1918–Sept. 1919 |
| G.18 | Vanessa | June 1918–Sept. 1919 |
| G.19 | Vanity | Sept. 1918–Sept. 1919 |
| G.20 | Valorous | Mar. 1918–Sept. 1919 |
| G.21 | Vortigern | |
| G.22 | Walker | post Jan.–Mar. 1918 |
| G.23 | Watchman | |
| G.24 | Viscount | Mar.–Sept. 1918 |
| G.25 | Valhalla | Jan.–Mar. 1918 |
| G.28 | Waterhen | Sept. 1918–Sept. 1919 |
| G.31 | Wrestler | June 1918–Sept. 1919 |
| G.33 | Wakeful | Uncertain |
| G.36 | Voyager | June 1918–Sept. 1919 |
| G.39 | Vivien | |
| G.40 | Wolsey | June 1918–Sept. 1919 |
| G.43 | Winchester | |
| G.45 | Valhalla | Mar. 1918–Sept. 1919 |
| G.46 | Stuart | post Sept. 1918–Sept. 1919 |
| G.50 | Vampire | Mar. 1918–Sept. 1919 |
| G.65 | Velox | post Sept. 1918–Sept. 1919 |
| G.70 | Vampire | |
| G.71 | Vivacious | Jan.–Mar. 1918 |
| G.73 | Whirlwind | |
| G.76 | Campbell | Nov. 1918–Sept. 1919 |
| G.96 | Warwick | Jan.–Sept. 1919 |
| G.98 | Venom | Sept. 1918–Sept. 1919 |

(renamed *Venomous* by June 1919)

FLAG SUPERIOR 'H'

| no. | ship | period used |
|---|---|---|
| H.0A | Vanquisher | |
| H.2A | Vehement | June 1918 et seq. |
| H.4A | Vanoc | |
| H.16 | Vimiera | Uncertain |
| H.33 | Vanoc | 1920–1940 |

| no. | ship | period used |
|---|---|---|
| H.38 | Watchman | |
| H.41 | Whitehall | Mar.–Sept. 1918 |
| H.43 | Velox | |
| H.55 | Vancouver | Uncertain |
| H.88 | Wakeful | |
| H.95 | Winchester | 1920–1938 |

FLAG SUPERIOR 'D'

| no. | ship | period used |
|---|---|---|
| D.00 | Stuart | |
| D.01 | Montrose | 1920–1940 |
| D.09 | Douglas | Nov. 1918 |
| D.19 | Malcolm | Nov. 1919–1940 |
| D.20 | Wallace | Sept. 1919–1938 |
| D.21 | Wryneck | Sept. 1919–1938 |
| D.22 | Waterhen | Sept. 1919–1940 |
| D.23 | Vimiera | post Oct. 1919–1940 |
| ,, | Walker | Sept.–Oct. 1919 |
| D.24 | Walrus | Sept. 1919–1938 |
| D.25 | Whirlwind | Sept.–Nov. 1918 |
| ,, | Warwick | |
| D.26 | Watchman | Sept. 1919–1940 |
| D.27 | Viceroy | Nov. 1919–1920 |
| ,, | Walker | 1920–1940 |
| ,, | Whirlwind | Sept.–Oct. 1919 |
| D.28 | Vanity | Sept. 1919–1938 |
| D.29 | Vanessa | Sept. 1919–1940 |
| D.30 | Woolston | Nov. 1919–1920 |
| ,, | Valorous | Sept.–Oct. 1919 |
| ,, | Whirlwind | 1920–1940 |
| D.31 | Voyager | Sept. 1919–1940 |
| D.32 | Viscount | Nov. 1919–1920 |
| ,, | Vivien | Sept.–Oct. 1919 |
| ,, | Versatile | 1920–1940 |
| D.33 | Vancouver | Sept. 1919–Apr. 1928 |
| ,, | Vimy (renamed) | Apr. 1928–1940 |
| D.34 | Velox | Sept. 1919–1940 |

FLAG SUPERIOR 'D'—*continued*

| no. | ship | period used |
|---|---|---|
| D.35 | Versatile | Sept.–Oct. 1919 |
| ,, | Wolsey | Nov. 1919–1920 |
| ,, | Wrestler | 1920–1938 |
| D.36 | Vivacious | } Sept. 1919–1940 |
| D.37 | Vortigern | |
| D.40 | Velox | Nov. 1918–Sept. 1919 |
| ,, | Spenser | Sept. 1919–1936 |
| D.41 | Walpole | Sept. 1919–1940 |
| D.42 | Windsor | } Sept. 1919–1940 |
| D.43 | Wessex | |
| D.44 | Wolfhound | Sept. 1919–1920 |
| ,, | Valhalla | 1920–1932 |
| D.45 | Westminster | Sept. 1919–1938 |
| D.46 | Winchelsea | } Sept. 1919–1940 |
| D.47 | Westcott | |
| D.48 | Vidette | |
| D.49 | Valentine | Sept. 1939–1938 |
| D.50 | Shakespeare | Sept. 1919–1936 |
| D.51 | Vectis | Sept. 1919–1936 |
| D.52 | Vega | Sept. 1919–1938 |
| D.53 | Venetia | Sept. 1919–1940 |
| D.54 | Vanquisher | Nov. 1919–1940 |
| ,, | Verulam | Sept. 1919 (already lost) |
| D.55 | Vesper | Sept. 1919–1940 |
| D.56 | Vimiera | Sept. 1919–1920 |
| ,, | Wolfhound | 1920–1938 |
| D.57 | Violent | Nov. 1919–1936 |
| D.60 | Campbell | Sept. 1919–1940 |
| D.61 | Valkyrie | 1920–1936 |
| ,, | Whitley | Sept. 1919–1920 |
| D.62 | Wrestler | Sept.–Oct. 1919 |
| ,, | Wild Swan | Nov. 1919–1940 |
| D.63 | Woolston | Sept.–Oct. 1919 |
| ,, | Verity | Nov. 1919–1940 |
| D.64 | Wolsey | Sept.–Oct. 1919 |
| ,, | Vansittart | Nov. 1919–1940 |
| D.65 | Wakeful | Sept. 1919–1920 |

| no. | ship | period used |
|------|------|-------------|
| D.66 | Winchester | Sept.–Oct. 1919 |
| ,, | Wivern | Nov. 1919–1940 |
| D.67 | Valkyrie | Sept.–Oct. 1919 |
| ,, | Wishart | Nov. 1919–1940 |
| D.68 | Valhalla | Sept.–Oct. 1919 |
| ,, | Vampire | Nov. 1919–1940 |
| D.69 | Vendetta | Sept. 1919–1940 |
| D.70 | Vampire | Sept.–Oct. 1919 |
| ,, | Mackay | Nov. 1919–1940 |
| D.71 | Verdun | Sept.–Oct. 1919 |
| ,, | Volunteer | Nov. 1919–1940 |
| D.72 | Veteran | Nov. 1919–1940 |
| D.73 | Viscount | Sept.–Oct. 1919 |
| ,, | Vivien | Nov. 1919–1938 |
| D.74 | Wanderer | June 1919–1940 |
| D.75 | Venomous | Nov. 1919–1940 |
| D.76 | Witherington | June 1919–1940 |
| D.77 | Whitshed | Nov. 1919–1940 |
| D.78 | Wolverine | July 1920–1940 |
| D.81 | Bruce | Nov. 1919–1939 |
| D.82 | Valorous | 1920–1938 |
| D.83 | Broke | } 1925–1940 |
| D.84 | Keppel | |
| D.87 | Venturous | 1920–1936 |
| D.88 | Wren | |
| D.89 | Witch | |
| D.90 | Douglas | |
| D.91 | Viceroy | |
| D.92 | Viscount | } 1920–1940 |
| D.93 | Verdun | |
| D.94 | Whitehall | |
| D.95 | Woolston | |
| D.96 | Worcester | |
| D.97 | Whitley | } 1920–1938 |
| D.98 | Wolsey | |
| D.3A | Wallace | } allotted during building |
| DA.6 | Mackay | |

FLAG SUPERIOR 'L'

| no. | ship | period used |
|-----|------|-------------|
| L.00 | Valorous | } 1938–1945 |
| L.02 | Wolsey | |
| L.04 | Wryneck | } 1938–1940 |
| L.10 | Westler | |
| L.21 | Viceroy | 1938–1945 |
| L.23 | Whitley | } 1938–1940 |
| L.29 | Vimiera | |
| L.33 | Vivien | |
| L.38 | Vanity | |
| L.40 | Westminster | |
| L.41 | Vega | } 1938–1945 |
| L.49 | Woolston | |
| L.55 | Winchester | |
| L.56 | Wolfhound | 1938–1940 |
| L.64 | Wallace | 1938–1945 |
| L.69 | Valentine | } 1938–1940 |
| L.91 | Wakeful | |
| L.93 | Verdun | } 1938–1945 |
| L.94 | Windsor | |

FLAG SUPERIOR 'I'

*Note*: This was, like Flag Superior 'L', reserved for escort destroyers, including the old American 'flush-deckers'. Many of the older destroyers and leaders exchanged Flag Superior 'D' for 'I', and the change took place early in 1940 in all cases. No further changes were made to the pendant numbers of destroyers listed.

| no. ship | no. ship | no. ship | no. ship |
|---|---|---|---|
| *I.00 Stuart* | *I.29 Vanessa* | *I.55 Vesper* | *I.76 Witherington* |
| *I.01 Montrose* | *I.30 Whirlwind* | *I.56 Wolfhound* | *I.77 Whitshed* |
| *I.19 Malcolm* | *I.31 Voyager* | (ex *L.56*) | *I.78 Wolverine* |
| *I.21 Wryneck* | *I.32 Versatile* | *I.60 Campbell* | *I.83 Broke* |
| (before | *I.33 Vimy* | *I.62 Wild Swan* | *I.84 Keppel* |
| conversion) | *I.34 Velox* | *I.63 Verity* | *I.88 Wren* |
| *I.22 Waterhen* | *I.36 Vivacious* | *I.64 Vansittart* | (uncertain) |
| *I.25 Warwick* | *I.37 Vortigern* | *I.66 Wivern* | *I.89 Witch* |
| (1940) | *I.41 Walpole* | *I.67 Wishart* | *I.90 Douglas* |
| *I.25 Vimiera* | *I.43 Wessex* | *I.68 Vampire* | *I.91 Viceroy* |
| (ex *L.29*) | *I.46 Winchelsea* | *I.69 Vendetta* | (ex *L.21*) |
| *I.26 Watchman* | *I.47 Westcott* | *I.70 Mackay* | *I.92 Viscount* |
| *I.27 Walker* | *I.48 Vidette* | *I.71 Volunteer* | *I.93 Verdun* |
| *I.28 Vanity* | *I.50 Wrestler* | *I.72 Veteran* | *I.94 Whitehall* |
| (before | (ex *L.10*) | *I.74 Wanderer* | *I.96 Worcester* |
| conversion) | *I.53 Venetia* | *I.75 Venomous* | (renamed |
| | *I.54 Vanquisher* | | *Yeoman* 1944) |

# BIBLIOGRAPHY
# AND SOURCE LIST

## PUBLISHED WORKS

*British Destroyers* (Putnam, 1961) by Capt. T. D. Manning C.B.E., V.R.D., R.N.V.R.

*British Destroyers* (Seeley Service, 1966) by Edgar J. March

*British Warships* (David & Charles, 1969) by J. J. Colledge

*Convoy Escort Commander* (Cassell, 1964) by Vice-Adm. Sir Peter Gretton, K.C.B., D.S.O., O.B.E., D.S.C.

*Greek Tragedy* (Antony Blond, 1964) by Anthony Heckstall-Smith and Vice-Adm. H. T. Baillie-Grohman

*Endless Story* (Hodder & Stoughton, 1931) by 'Taffrail'

*The Nine Days of Dunkirk* (Faber & Faber, 1959) by David Divine

*Royal Australian Navy, 1939–45*, Vols. I–II, by C. Hermon Gill

*The War at Sea*, Vols. I–III (H.M.S.O., 1954–1961), by S. W. Roskill

*Warships of World War II* (Ian Allan, 1964) by H. T. Lenton & J. J. Colledge

*U-boats Sunk* (Putnam, 1958) by Robert M. Grant

*U-Boat Killer* (Weidenfeld & Nicolson, 1956) by Capt. D. Macintyre, D.S.O.**, D.S.C., R.N.

## OFFICIAL RECORDS

'Pink Lists' (Dispositions of H.M. Ships)—Admiralty Library

Ships' Covers (P.R.O. reference ADM 138)—National Maritime Museum

Ships' Histories (P.R.O. reference ADM 137)—Public Record Office

Ships' Plans—National Maritime Museum

*Ships' Photographs*—Imperial War Museum Collection, Ministry of Defence Collection and National Maritime Museum Collection, etc., and as credited